The **Chaplain** is **In**:
Journey to Health and Happiness

Chaplain Joy Le Page Smith, M.A.

Copyright © 2013 Joy Le Page Smith

Printed in the United States of America

Pathways to Healing – Ministries of Joy

All rights reserved. No part of this publication may be reproduced, stored in a retrieval system, or transmitted in any form or by any means electronic, mechanical, photocopying, recording or otherwise, without the prior written permission of the author.

ISBN-13: 978-0615761893
ISBN-10: 0615761895

Cover and interior book design by Janelle Mahler.

All Scripture quotations, unless otherwise indicated, are from the Holy Bible: NKJV.

This Book is Dedicated To

my husband, Gary Smith, our three sons
Ted, Tim and Todd

Also To:

EACH PERSON WHO READS IN HOPES FOR
GROWTH AND WHOLENESS.

Life as it rolls
is a little damaged...
a little imperfect.
What matters is
what we learn and
what we pass on to others
as love grows in our souls.

ACKNOWLEDGMENTS

Each person seen by me, as a chaplain, contributed to my life and therefore to the writing of this book. When we give, we receive–and I have received a lot of love. My greatest joy comes in witnessing the results when people take the needs of their hearts seriously. My thanks go to all who have honored me with their trust. Now, I say with a full heart: *your presence in my life has made this book possible.*

I especially acknowledge my husband Gary's faithful support and diligence in making sure the book was ready for publishing. He was my daily encourager, believing in the finished product even before it was finished. Thank you, "Gary the Great," my soul mate for all the hours you have read and edited my work through the years.

I thank Dr. Brent Leathers for his knowledge and expertise he poured into the creation of this book. He never showed impatience with my need to lean on his skills and mentoring. Friends and associates who read portions of the manuscript or helped in other ways include Dr. Leslie Edison, Jonathan Massey, Michael Traub, Linda Milot, Rae Ann Proost, Chery Kitchens, Colette Cowman, and Bobbie Sofia. Their encouragement and suggestions held me on target with the task. A special thanks goes to my family, clients and friends whose prayers undergirded the work. Last, but far from least I am grateful to Janelle Mahler. Credit is due for her excellent skills in formatting, photography and graphics.

FOREWORD

Chaplains are ministers who serve in specialized settings such as hospitals, prisons, hospices, and the military. Joy Le Page Smith, a certified chaplain and author, works within a doctor's office, merging mental health counseling and spiritual direction. Her work was featured as a cover story in *Vision*, entitled "The Chaplain is In." This publication for chaplains celebrated Joy's private practice in chaplaincy as "pioneering." Now, she uses *The Chaplain is In: Journey to Health and Happiness* as the title of her book.

For the past ten years, Joy has been my spiritual director. She has seen me through many disappointments, trials, and doubts. As a spiritual director myself, it has been vital to experience regular direction. I am grateful that God brought Joy Smith into my life. And, I am grateful that she has now taken the time to share many of her insights, as well as much of her life story, with all of us on the printed page. She speaks from her own experience as she says, "It is God's longing that we have an *intimate* relationship with Him."

Along with many others, Joy went through a tumultuous journey on the way to discovering this relationship, a journey which vividly shows God's transformative process at work in her. Tremendous trials served to prepare her to bring compassion and fortitude to others, thereby blessing their lives. Joy works with people just like us. We can see our own reflections in the mirror from the case studies woven throughout her book. And, just as God was there for Joy, she is now here for us.

The Chaplain is In: Journey to Health and Happiness is the story of a person who overcame huge obstacles on the way to enjoying an intimate relationship with God. Wherever you are on your path to God, to health, to happiness, you will benefit greatly by the wisdom contained within this book.

Jonathan Massey, M.Div.
December 2012

PREFACE

Do you doubt your worth, regret your past or feel thwarted by hurts perpetrated by others? These dilemmas can create a perpetual sense of uselessness or overwhelming defeat. Are we *good enough, doing* enough--or getting far enough in life? If this strikes home for you, you are not alone. Sufferings of this and other kinds of pain are endured, at times, as part of being human. *The Chaplain Is In* provides helpful insights to assist you in restoring your self-worth and facing your challenges head-on. Together, we will get you through to what lies on the other side of these challenging questionings that can shake one's faith. There is a freedom, a peace, and a joy ahead to be savored. This book can help you find it.

The words of a song "Something beautiful, something good, all my confusion He understood," are treasured. Why? Because that is my life. From a woman who wanted to die--and tried to commit suicide, I arose from the fires of life. My body itself insisted on death...many times God won out. No, I was to live. A plan and a purpose lie ahead. A love for God and His Word brought me through every pull toward the grave. I yearned for more, wondering how something beautiful, something good could come from me. If you have ever doubted your worth or wondered about your identity, this book has much to offer.

God did not forsake my wondering. Time and training came next. Today, as a certified chaplain I stand at bedsides, in trauma centers, and with prisoners. Why did all this happen? Because God would not leave me alone. I *had to* front and center--nothing else would do. It was as if God said, "No! I won't let you go!" Nothing other than moving onward and upward, on the wings of the Spirit, would do. God's plan lifted me high above past fears within emotional and physical dilemmas. As these came and went, God said to my soul, "You will live. And, I will come alive in you!" So, the longing grew: I had to let the living God do His work in me--one hundred percent. It was "do or die."

As my soul yearned for more and more of God, I had to let go all guilt due to weaknesses and failures. A vision of living the life God was offering crescendoed. Truths found in the Bible became like thermals pulling me higher, so I could rise up and embrace the fullness, the peace, and the joy God has for *all His people*. *There is more ... than we ever dreamed. We are created to be expressions of God's presence on earth.*

I love the story of the rising Phoenix. From the fires of life lay ashes at my feet. Yet, out of those ashes comes a heart that carries *that fire* that lights my way while walking alongside those who are in the worst kinds of pain and suffering. It is my *desire* to bring God's helps to them that *makes me able* to *see and hear* their pain.

Mostly, chaplains are thought to serve within the military. Even more of us serve in hospitals, hospices, prisons and jails. These places become our battlegrounds. The weapon we carry is God's loving, listening Presence. Yes, even *in me--the weakling!*

And, yes, here am I...one who lived through what seemed like perpetual bouts with my body's determination to die. Yet, with God's healing in my soul and His fire alive in my bones, I can carry hope, comfort, and love to those who are under fire while dodging the bullets of life—or have fallen into pits while trying to "make a life."

Truth be known: God has power to *do even more in and through you!* I write so that you, too, will see your strength, your beauty--and arise. Arise, from whatever it is that holds you back. For, there is healing in His wings" (Mal 4:2). Finding the healing we want and need is part and parcel to this book. *The chaplain is in!*

Contents

Pastoral Incident # 1 2
Chapter One 6
Pastoral Incident # 2 19
Chapter Two 24
Pastoral Incident # 3 37
Chapter Three 42
Pastoral Incident # 4 54
Chapter Four 58
Pastoral Incident # 5 70
Chapter Five 74
Chapter Six 87
Addendums 97

The Chaplain is in: Journey to Health and Happiness

Pastoral Incident # 1

As I enter the woman's hospital room, I am tired. Still, several more hours of patient work lay ahead. Fortunately, this person is welcoming. She asks me to sit. As is often the case in chaplaincy, this will be our only encounter. I will call her Mrs. A.[1]

Mrs. A. spends nearly an hour telling me of the chest pain that brings her to the hospital. Plans are in place for her to be released later in the day. She seems nearly frantic to get home. After she talks out some of her frustrations with hospital life, Mrs. A. becomes calmer. Before long, she allows me into the deeper places of her life.

"Tell me about what interests you most," I ask.

"Well, I have no family nearby. My children live in other states. I don't get to see them much." She gazes out the window for long moments, then sighs before adding, "They have their own lives to live, you know."

"Do they visit you?"

She laughed, but the edge in her voice negates any real humor. "They planned to come last year, but that didn't pan out. I've asked them every year. My daughter says it is easier and less expense for me to travel to see them. My son is always going to visit me, but something inevitably comes up for either him or his wife. So, except for one brief stay years ago, they haven't made any trips to see me."

"Are you planning to visit them?"

"No. I guess I'm kind of a homebody." There is a long silence before she sighs again, then says, "Chaplain Joy, I am an alcoholic."

---

[1] When names or initials are used within this book these have been changed to protect the privacy of individuals. Circumstances are also changed, within this writing, to assure individuals are not identified.

"Thank you for your honesty. How long has this been true for you?"

"I started drinking soon after my husband died. And, I am not able to stop. Alcohol is what holds me together."

Mrs. A. tells of her husband's death ten years ago. As we talk further, it is evident she has not known how to grieve the loss of her husband. They were married 25 years. As her story unfolds, it is clear that Mrs. A. fears her tears.

"I cried at the funeral, of course. Then the tears went on for days. I was afraid."

"What was the fear about?"

"I felt totally unnerved by the tears. I was afraid I would not be able to stop crying. I feared losing control. My memory was bad...my thoughts were so disconnected. I thought I was going crazy."

"You are describing what the stress of grief is like for a person when it is new."

"I guess so. But, I wasn't going to take a chance. I had to soothe myself in a different way. At first, I was only drinking one vodka tonic in the afternoons to get through the day. Soon, I needed more. It was not long before I was drinking throughout the day and evening."

I explain, "People hide from their grief in different ways. You use alcohol. Some people get more and more involved in work or frantic play. You are not alone. Many people don't want to think about what they've lost. They dread their grief."

Mrs. A. begins to understand. She says, "I tried not to feel how much I missed Roger. I guess I was trying not to pay attention to what I felt. I've been hiding my feelings in a vodka bottle. Now, I'm here with a heart attack!"

"Would you like to know a better way of grieving?"

She says "yes" to this, so I explain that grief has two parts. "The first part involves attending to the hurt that is present inside. There is great pain in losing a person from your life. Significant adjustments stand before you as your days are no longer the same. Although people don't want to feel the pain, giving place to it is vitally important. The second part of grief work comes through mourning as the sadness arises. Mourning involves talking about your loss–and the person you have lost–with trusted others. Allow your tears. They will help you heal. Moving into the grief when the tears are felt, then out of it, allows you to not get overwhelmed, such as you have feared. The process gets easier as you go through it. Some people find help through attending a grief group."

Before our time together ends, she can see clearly that avoiding her grief brings her to the place where she is now. We pray together for her to be able to honor her grief and to do the work it takes to resolve it in a healthy way. We ask God for healing in her life and that she can find meaning while living it out as a single woman, doing things that nurture her.

"You will learn to see how that sadness visits, then lifts, as you honor it by allowing yourself to feel the pain of your losses. This is the opposite of putting a wall between you and your tears. This is different from hiding from pain by numbing out through using alcohol. Trust the process. It works."

Mrs. A. accepts my counsel of not expecting to quickly resolve the pain of losing her husband. "Chaplain Joy, I see what you are saying. I know I didn't grieve and I want to change that." She pauses before continuing, "There is no way I can live the way I've been going."

I end the encounter, saying, "Before you leave the hospital, I will prepare two lists for you. One list will include several grief groups that you may want to choose to visit. Feel free to visit each of them before deciding which group is best for your needs. The second list will offer several locations in this city where A.A. groups meet. Alcoholics Anonymous has helped millions of people worldwide over generations of time. You may want to include this avenue of care, as you learn more about handling your emotions. I feel confident that if you take these steps, you will find the help you need. And, don't be surprised if your physical health is affected positively as a result, especially if you also develop one or two things that truly interest you in life. My dear lady, you are worth every possible effort to be the person you most want to be."

Hope fills her eyes as she takes my hand and asks me to continue praying for her. When our eyes open, they are wet. My heart is touched by her story. We hug. With more understanding of herself and her needs, Mrs. A's life can be different.

As I leave her room and walk toward the next patient encounter, I pray inwardly for her to embrace the path extended toward emotional healing, and to begin a recovery program from alcoholism.

Chapter One

"Christ has paid the price to set us free, but many Christians are not free. They are bound by compulsions or problems such as fear, grief, hurt, anxiety, suicidal thoughts, anger, lust, hate, sickness, or other emotional disorders."
Dr. Colin Warren

In reading the above quote, one might agree, yet ask *where does all that "junk" come from*? Dr. Eugene Wiesner, a friend who is a psychologist, says compulsions and the like come from "poor potty training." It is his way of helping people realize that events from childhood affect their adulthood, creating difficult feelings. This is also true of the memories that are attached to times when, as a child, we were confined, confused, frustrated, disappointed and, at points, punished.

As adults, these experiences leave us with undesirable impulses and unwanted urges that can surface at any moment. If life holds mostly chaos, lacks purpose, or we don't feel complete, our psyches need some deep healing. Remember, too, that the subconscious mind is holding images of *everything* that ever happened to us. It is a wonderful gift from God that we don't have to deal with all that at once! It is, however, the subconscious that presents tiny segments of thought persisting as pop-ups within our daily endeavors. Some people call this activity "the monkey mind," as these segments of thought can jump and fly around in our minds with great speed.

That which is in our subconscious mind is hard to reach. Within the average person's quest for healing, it is okay to leave it there. For those who want or need to go deeper, it will take the help of a professional to find the "burrs under the saddle" of the subconscious mind. If we are serious about emotional and spiritual growth—and if we are paying attention—God will help us see what needs addressing for the sake of healing. He will make way for our inner healing to the degree we are ready to cooperate. Some of us earnestly desire to be all we can be for the purpose of growth and for the glory of God. God will take us to a place where, for sure, we see all we need to see and reach all we need to reach. Until then, we will deal more peripherally with what is commonly known as our distinguishable "baggage."

Most of us have baggage of which we are quite conscious. This involves elements of behavior that we would like very much to forget. Patterns acquired in childhood are very strong. We may spend years ignoring them and trying to just *forgetaboutit*! "Move on" is the message we give ourselves. *After all, there are a lot of other things to think about.* So, the emotions are gulped down and the patterns ignored.

Yet, repressing difficult emotions, both past and present, is not practical as they do not go away. They remain deep inside and cause havoc at points in life. Buried emotions can even play a role in creating some of life's most difficult problems: alcoholism, addictions of various sorts, failed relationships, perpetually low self-esteem, and even physical illness.

In the "Pastoral Incident," Mrs. A. feared her emotions, since she didn't know where they would take her. She had a hard lesson to learn: If we don't deal with our grief, our grief will deal with us. It is always fear that makes us run from our emotions. And, it is not unusual for fear to arise when we consider talking with someone about what we feel. Those of us who do reach out for help, and revisit the places in life that hurt the most, find we are greatly helped. Granted, there are lots of things we would rather do. For some of us, trusting another with the secrets of our psyches does not come easy. Pushing past that wall of fear and distrust, however, is how we break old patterns that stymie us. Now, we can build new patterns. In doing so we gain better understanding and appreciation of ourselves. This enables us to validate our emotions. Amazing gains come as a result of this inner healing work as health improves: mentally, emotionally, physically, and spiritually.

Not everyone needs a professional to gain skills in valuing their emotions and attending to them appropriately. A psychotherapist once told me, "If everyone had one trustworthy friend to talk to when times get tough, I would be out of business." But, what happens if you don't have such a friend? Books can be mighty friends. For expediting inner healing, I recommend David Seamands' *Healing Damaged Emotions*.[2] This book, translated into over 15 languages, extends an outstanding Scriptural approach to gaining emotional healing.

I know from personal experience that, at times, it is important to get the help of a professional. A part of my own story is hard to share; yet, it is included here to witness to the fact that sometimes the help of professionals is essential. Our psyches can get stuck so tight as to become immobile, like a truck in the mud! I extend my story here knowing it may reach readers who are in great turmoil at this very moment, needing to know God is especially with them when they are in the deepest kind of pain.

I was in my 20's when I reached that point. After eight years of marriage, I realized there was no good choice other than to divorce my husband. At the time, it was difficult for a woman to receive a divorce decree from the judicial system. It took a very long time before a judge granted me that piece of paper. By the time the judgment came down allowing me to divorce, I was in a state of high anxiety. At night, I would awaken with terror ringing like a giant bell in my mind.

During my eight years of marriage, I gave birth to three little boys. They were the joy of my life; yet serious challenges now faced me

---

[2] David Seamands, *Healing Damaged Emotions* (Ontario: David C. Cook, 1981).

and the children. Some of those challenges seemed insurmountable. Keeping dependable, trustworthy childcare for eight to nine hours while I worked, was close to impossible. I had little peace leaving them with another. I got less and less sleep.

As I lay awake, I thought about my church and long-term friends. But, my divorce was deemed wrong among the church leadership. I no longer felt welcome, and leaving brought plenty of tears. Even today, I miss that wonderful church. At the time, I thought they were the experts with Scripture, and their words, "God hates divorce," landed like a blast of fire in my mind each time I heard it.

Eventually, new friends and new adventures, like drinking and dancing, began during the weekends when the boys were with their father. I enjoyed these experiences to a point, but I worried, knowing I was moving far beyond the land of contentment I had once known. The experiences of relating with God as a child were real, yet now far out of reach.

My marriage was complicated enough, but my health was unstable as well. Periodic episodes of blood clots traveling from my legs and abdomen into my heart and lungs were life-threatening. No medical reason could be found for this deadly condition. All the doctors could do was work to save my life within each of these traumatic events and keep me on Coumadin, a blood thinner. I knew dependence on God was what brought me through numerous blood clot episodes. I feared another episode of traveling blood clots would come—another time of calling an ambulance. Another hospital stay. I had no health insurance. I worried about my children. If I became hospitalized again, how would that affect them? Who would care for them? These were real concerns...but I was *worrying myself sick*! At the same time, I am living outside the church, seeking pleasure in ways I never considered in the past.

My conscience prodded me like the point of a hot poker, reminding me of my earlier moorings. Disappointing the people I loved since childhood was a hard burden to bear. They were the ones who prayed me through times of being near death during blood clot events! Deciding to divorce had now placed me in a different light with the people of the church. In their eyes, I was "backslidden."

God was trying to pull me back. And, I was resisting. I could forget all the hurt of the past, after a couple of drinks, while out with this new crowd. Trouble came in the fact I didn't know any one of these new friends well enough to talk out what was going on inside. The pattern of "canning" my emotions since childhood now saw all of those emotions coming up, screaming for attention!

One evening I dialed my doctor, thinking there was something he could do to help me. I could tell when he answered the phone he was disturbed by receiving this evening call. Self-doubt came crashing in. I thought calling him would be okay. He was an *elder in our church*, after all!

I brought my mind front-and-center again, then said, "I am having a horribly difficult time with anxiety, Dr. M. I think I am having a nervous breakdown."

A big sigh came across the line. Then he said, "I guess that's up to you."

After waiting long moments for him to say more, nothing came. Finally, I hung up the phone to ponder what that meant. It didn't take long to surmise that he, too, was judging me for having a divorce! Why else would a doctor fail to extend even a few words for managing anxiety? This was in the 1960s, a time when many, if not most, doctors doubted that psychiatrists and psychologists had a valid place in medicine. Later, medications became more available. Now, doctors regularly treat patients for anxiety and depression by prescribing medications when these conditions are unmanageable. Even though I understand this, I still wonder how a doctor could be cold, abrupt, and uncaring with a person so obviously in great pain.

While in the church, there were always trusted people to talk with before or after service. These people were happy to pray with anyone who needed help. But, I couldn't go back. *I was divorced*, after all! Now, "out of God's will," or so I believed. At least, I knew that was what my congregation believed.

Pride was involved. Mom and Dad tried to talk me out of

marrying at age 17. They were unsure about the person I chose to marry. So, going home to cry to them was out of the picture. No, I would somehow make it alone.

No one seemed available to help me break through the huge amount of anguish that had built over those eight years of marriage that rocked my soul and broke my spirit. The desire to die came alive when I was at my weakest. I felt guilty for going against my church, a church that served as my lifeline from ages eight to twenty-three. Although alcohol beaconed, it didn't have a firm hold on me. Had I been exposed to mind-altering drugs, I may have chosen one to escape my mounting sorrow. I had spent most of my life in church prior to this, so exploring what the rest of the world used to help them with their anguish was foreign to me.

I remember the day when the load of my losses and the concern for my three children brought me low. I felt beat down. Lost. Without hope. I tried not to think of God. Surely, He would want to punish me. There was a sense of being truly washed up. I began to feel the burden, realizing the chore of *managing myself* was getting too great! Thoughts of having sidetracked my values and failed my children pressed upon me with greater force with each passing day. *How can I be a good mother to these children whom I love so much? It appears I can no longer do them justice. What will happen to them if I keep getting sick and can't take care of them?* Shame and guilt over divorcing my husband and no longer being in the church pounded me like storm-driven waves. These thoughts were hammering me. I couldn't make them stop.

In that state of mind, I decided it was best to end my life. I was sure my plan would not fail. I knew if I took enough Coumadin, the medication I was on for preventing further blood clots, I would bleed out from every orifice of my body. The doctor had warned me that Coumadin was a deadly medication, one that required frequent blood testing in order to stay in a safe range with it.

First, I arranged for my three little sons to be taken from the house so they would not see the traumatic results of my plan. *This way, they will only hear about it,* I told myself.

Many claim suicide is a selfish act. Perhaps it is, in some cases. But, judging is unfair. It is impossible to know what happens to a person's mind when that person becomes so emotionally sick as to *need to die*. I was there. Yet, within what would have been my last hour of life, God intervened in two ways. For one, the person who picked up my children sensed I needed help and called a family member who, in turn, phoned my parents. My father happened to be home that afternoon with two visiting friends. So, when the call came, Dad and his friends came directly to my home to determine what was happening.

They found me sitting on my bed with a handful of Coumadin. I don't know how long I sat there trying to take the pills. The fact that *I could not move my arm* was the second intervening factor. As hard as I tried, it was as if my arm froze in mid-air. The pills were so close, yet I could not get them to my mouth. When Dad entered my bedroom my arm was out-stretched. Over 20 deadly pills lay in my hand. I wanted the pills. I wanted death. But, instead, I sat still as a stone.

My father stepped close, then gently said, "Joy, hand me the pills." My hand moved immediately and met his as I released the Coumadin. I am here today to love and serve my family, friends, and others because of these amazing interventions.

People cared, and help quickly arrived. In looking back, I see how the emotional sickness crept up on me without my realizing where I was headed. I also see how the Great Shepherd was with me right there in the valley of near death. In retrospect, I believe my misery would not have been so soul-shattering had friends from the church walked alongside me after my divorce. No doubt, it seemed natural for me to walk it alone, based on my pattern of keeping the hardest parts of life to myself.

Writing the above brings back those bitter memories of alienation. However, God showed love to me following those difficult times. I am always thrilled in remembering one early morning when I awakened to hear a choir of angels singing the hymn "Abide with me." My spirit met the music and soared! What an awesome happening! In an instant, I knew what this meant. God was not punishing me. Instead, the *beautiful* music and words of the song were saying, "I am here to love you." My heart leaped as I joyfully thought *God wants me to walk with Him again*! The next thoughts were ones of doubt: *How could this be true? How could He love me this much? Did I really hear angels singing? Maybe the boys got up and turned on the television. That might be what I heard?* So, I got up to see. No. Each boy was sleeping soundly in his bed. *Hooray! It is true! Regardless of all, I am loved*! Very soon after that I found a church where I felt welcomed as a divorcee.

During the two years after my near-suicide, I achieved two things. I began my inner-healing journey with professional help. Then, I entered a one-year training program and became certified as a medical secretary. Soon, I had a more dependable and promising way to earn my living. I moved slowly, but solidly, on course for letting go the aftermath of divorce, and the rocky ground of a break down.

The time had come for meeting and marrying a wonderful man, Gary Smith. He took on this family of four (the children were age four, seven, and nine) showing no hesitation in face of the changes this covenant would bring to his life. Today, my three sons are all adults, and two of them have children of their own. All three sons are strong, Christian men. They saw Gary's example, looked up to him, and called him "Dad" very early on. Through him, my sons know what it means to be integritous and courageous. God provided this man to join us in life. With him, all four of us could learn and grow. For sure, it is because of Gary's supportive, loving heart that I have been able to gain the education and credentialing needed to do the work of a chaplain and mental health counselor. It seems clear our allegiance supports one another's growth.

Before Gary's love, I heard it said that "God loves unconditionally." I could not comprehend this. It took finding that kind of love though Gary; then I could comprehend "unconditional love." Gary was able to handle everything that was difficult about me–taking all within an even stride. Even the episodes of blood clots that came during our early years together did not thwart him.

While in my 30s, and now remarried, I knew I had to address my unresolved grief. I realized it was coming out in my body through physical illness. After reading multiple medical articles that showed the connection between the psyche and physical health, I became convinced of the relationship between my several illnesses and my continued pattern of failing to acknowledge and validate my emotions. I began an earnest quest to comprehend *how* events experienced earlier in life were still affecting me, preventing me from having good health. I was ready and willing to do whatever I could in order to be well. This meant revisiting the pain of the past and dealing with difficult emotions.

My life experiences showed me that most doctors pay little, if any, attention to what goes on in a patient's psyche. Mostly, in the past, they were taught to diagnosis conditions and illnesses while treating with medicine and therapy without consideration of the psyche. This is changing. A number of physicians are now embracing the findings of a new field in medicine, called psychoneuroimmunology. Research within this fairly new field of study is making it clear within the medical arena that *what goes on in a person's psyche* affects the body's immune system, neurological system and endocrine system. The mind, the will, and the emotions of patients (elements of the soul) are considered more important than ever to astute doctors who value the research psychoneuroimmunology (PNI) reveals. They give attention to *more than* what the physical body is presenting upon an examination. What is happening in the person's life is also important to their care. I rejoice in knowing that doctors are currently referring patients to counselors, psychologists, or psychiatrists, when appropriate, based on the symptoms they see. In this way, people are more likely to get all the help they need for attending to the matters of the psyche (soul).

Years passed. Then in my late 40s, I began my residency as a chaplain at Good Samaritan Regional Medical Center, I was elated to discover the advancement of psychoneuroimmunology (PNI) within the medical community! By this time, *I had already lived out* what those studies were showing. For, after eight years of doing inner healing work, I was no longer throwing blood clots to my heart and lungs!

Knowing the desperation that can drive a person to the edge of insanity created a desire in me to help people who are at that point—or *before* they arrive there. I understand the inner agony and what it is like to feel *less than* others. May God bless Ethel Waters for her words, "God don't make no junk." When one's soul feels like junk, and perhaps looks like junk to others, God takes the soul and creates a work of art. "Something beautiful, something good," (as Bill and Gloria Gaither's lyrics go). Today, as I work with people, I am able to stand tall and strong when facing the worst kinds of trouble within trauma centers, emergency rooms, death beds, and prison cells. It is God who saved my life, turned it around and built this strength in me.

The Latin for "psyche" is "soul." The Greek comprehension of the psyche (from which this Latin word comes) indicates "life, breathe, soul." My chaplaincy practice aligns with that understanding. For the past 18 years, I have been fortunate to work alongside an amazing doctor who believes that tending to the matters of the soul gives a person a better life and increases the body's ability to heal. When Dr. Edison met me nearly two decades ago, she invited me to work with her in her practice at Moon Valley Medical Center. She is a doctor who includes the findings of PNI in her practice. Dr. Edison knows the emotional, mental, and spiritual aspects of her patients' lives affect their physical health.

Before referring patients, Dr. Edison prepares them to know my work will involve their spiritual health, their griefs, and their emotional struggles. She knows these can easily be related to what is happening in their physical bodies. Many patients begin to understand the "whats" and "whys" of their troubling circumstances as we work together. Some find they need to make major changes in their lives. It is a matter of weighing all things so we can get to the bottom of what is disturbing them. Now, a new level of peace and joy, along with improved physical health, can be reached.

Within this work, I can see clearly that each of us plays a major role in our mental, emotional, and spiritual health. What we think and what we feel is more important than most of us realize. Our physical health is greatly affected by what is going on in our psyches (souls). Clearly, we do not have a healthy psyche when we carry bitterness, multiple fears, or buried sorrow. I shall never forget the poignant moments spent with Mrs. A., whose heart failed her when alcohol was chosen as a better solution for her sorrow than to earnestly involve herself with her losses.

The majority of people who come to me are referred by either a doctor or a minister. They enter my door totally undone, or close to it. My work is to help them as they grieve their losses, and adjust to major personal challenges. I teach clients about the Lord's desire to walk with them, during circumstances that seen unmanageable. Many are struck hard enough by life events to open an inner pool of mental and emotional toxicity previously unreached. This is "a place" where we can do our work.

Having worked for years with people who are in trouble with their emotions, I've pondered what happened to mine that found me so able to consider suicide in my twenties. The saying "the secrets of the soul are the cancers of the psyche" almost proved terminal. I grew up not expecting emotional support from my parents. Therefore, I learned to keep everything inside. My pattern was to numb out when trouble came. I am sure I carried that into my first marriage as a 17-year-old. Then, as the pressure built, my psyche reached an impasse that only God could surpass.

A minister once told me, "If parents were perfect, children would grow up worshiping them, instead of finding their own need to connect with God." What a piece of truth! Overcoming life's pain and struggles strengthens us and develops godly character when we depend on God to help us through every event, every obstacle. Jesus knows we carry heavy loads at times. He addresses this, saying, "Come to Me, all you who labor and are heavy laden, and I will give you rest" (Mt 11:28.) Maybe you can think of a time when you were there? Or, perhaps you are there right now?

There is a certain peace and freedom that can come in the midst of our struggles and sufferings as we face our fears and then release them. This is a freedom that grows more and more as we walk in faith with God. A friend, Dr. Brent Leathers, recently said, "I capitalize the word 'Faith.' I do that to emphasize its direct relation to God—a relation so close that when we have 'Faith' we have 'God' with us in a very real sense." Dr. Leathers is a theologian who thinks of "Faith" and "God" as being essentially "one-and-the-same," as long as that Faith is truly God-centered. So, living "in Faith" means living "in God."

When we bring "Faith" into a situation, we bring "God" to that circumstance. It is not our role to presuppose what God will do in any given situation, but rather to simply watch, with a trusting heart, what God is already doing. With gratefulness we can wait and trust.

We are not going to maintain this full measure of Faith all the time. But, we can seek to enter into it more and more fully. Given time and effort, we can find ourselves blocking all thoughts that are not Faith-based. This does take diligence and dedication, along with accepting ourselves during times when we *fail to maintain* the Faith that we know is intended for us. Living in Faith equates with enjoying levels of emotional and spiritual freedom, which are otherwise unattainable!

Jesus made the claim that, *if really lived out,* His teaching would set us free (Jn. 8:31-32). What keeps us from being fully dedicated to Christ's teachings? Often it is fear of what others will say or think about us. We also fear what might happen if we put our trust completely in Christ. We want to control all outcomes. Yet, God calls us to let go and let Him lead the way...let Him clear the path and comfort us when we are troubled. Jesus referred to this as being like a little child, with trusting loving parents. We know that, for some, the trust placed in our biological parents creates challenges to overcome. How wonderful it is to know that God is always at work turning our difficulties "to good," as we see in the promise of Romans 8:28. *God is bringing us into new life,* as only the perfect father can do. When we trust Him, we find our Father knows best. It takes dedication and commitment to get there, but we can have that child-like Faith. This is how to reach full freedom in one's spirit.

For years I pondered the Scripture passage, "Therefore, if anyone is in Christ, [he is] a new creation; old things have passed away; behold, all things have become new" (2 Cor. 5:17). I wondered why I couldn't become a new creation at the moment of trusting Christ as my Savior. Wasn't I "born again?" Now, I believe that, in part, it is a matter of needing to get honest with the hurts of life and get healed through doing our inner work. The other part lies with the fact that it takes time and experience to see all the places in ourselves that we need to see: selfishness, greed, prejudices, pessimisms, grudges, jealousies, resentments, bitterness, gossip, and manipulation of others, while attempting to control situations. That is a partial list of "me first" indicators. All these need surrendering–and more! We can't do that until we see these things in ourselves.

Scripture tells us to be "watchful over your spirit" (Mal. 2:16 from Young's Literal Translation). The only way to do that is to continually examine ourselves with the Holy Spirit's help. God patiently waits and is there for us as we do this work. And, because God is God, He sees us as *a fully new creation*. His vision of us *sees* the completed work *although we are not yet there*. Ponder that!

That is why I find just as many Christians complain of suffering anxiety and depression as do non-Christians. (Including all the oppositions Dr. Collin Warren listed in his quote at the beginning of this chapter.) My work involves teaching people to get into this work with their whole being, reaching all the *pay dirt* within the nook-and-crannies of the psyche, while consecrating every area of life and every attitude we have to the Lord. We cannot suppress the grievous things that happen, or the incompleteness of ourselves, by merely saying "it's all good." No. We have to reach and work through the pain of being a work in progress, because *it is not all good*. Hiding from what is deep inside finds us affected by it, mostly in subtle ways–and lots of time within relationships. It is for sure that we have to attend to our patterns and grieve our losses to become "fully free and fully alive," as John Powell put it. This is the kind of freedom the Lord wants for us.

Joy Le Page Smith

Pastoral Incident # 2

The doctor calls for a chaplain to see the patient in room 210. He says, "This woman is having severe pain in her stomach, yet I've done every possible test without finding a cause."

When I arrive in her room she is curled up in a ball and does not appear to want my presence. I sit in a chair nearby. Time passes. Inwardly, I pray for wisdom, as compassion is already there. In time, she faces me. I say, "Your doctor tells me you have a lot of pain."

She says, "Yes, I do. But he isn't able to help me. All my tests are coming back normal."

I see her eyes are beginning to well up with tears. "Tell me about yourself," I ask.

"Well, I'm in my sixties. These were supposed to be my Golden Years."

"Aside from being sick, right now, what are you finding enjoyable in life?"

"Nothing." Now, tears are slowly making little paths on her cheeks.

"Are you retired?"

"I was forced to leave work."

"What does it mean to you to be forced to stop working?"

"It is hell! That's what it is," she says with great fervor. "I think that is why I'm in this hospital bed!"

For the next hour, the woman reveals her story. Her elderly mother became ill two years before. There is no other family member who can take care of her mother except this daughter. She speaks of feeling saddled with a situation she has no way of avoiding. Now, her face hardens as her history spills out. Her mother abused her while she was a child. No measure of a meaningful relationship developed between them. Tears begin to actively flow. I wait, knowing there is more. Yes, now the sobs are coming as she tells of being a Christian, yet holding hate for her mother all these years.

"I tried to care for her...but those memories just kept coming back. I never felt safe around her. Even as an adult, she pushed my buttons. I think she must have enjoyed it!"

Sobbing begins again. Many tears have accumulated through a lifetime of resenting this mother. Here, in the hospital, she faces her sorrow full throttle.

"Have you ever talked to anyone about this?" I ask.

"No. I've been too ashamed to admit this. It is something I can't get over."

"What about your pastor. Do you think it could be time to let your pastor in on this?"

"No!" She nearly shouts. I am a deacon in my church. Please understand! I cannot go to him!"

"OK, I understand that. You said earlier that you believe your stomach pain has to do with the care you feel duty-bound to give your mother. It is obvious a lot of emotion is present as regards this relationship. Would you like to pray with me for a healing of those painful memories?"

"Yes. But first...I need to tell you how sorry I am for what I have done." Silence follows. I know not to talk when there is this kind of a pause. She is gathering the courage to go on.

"I have been hitting my mother."

"Oh," I say. While taking this in I'm searching for words. A big breath is needed as I realize this confession carries as much guilt and shame for this patient as it took courage to tell me.

I tell her, "I am so sorry. This is a lot of pain for you, isn't it?"

She covers her mouth, then says, "Oh, yes! And, I've finally told someone. I hate myself for doing this—and I am afraid I will do it again!"

Knowing that within this hospital we are a team and that we will not let that happen again to this woman's mother, I continue here. I can extend to her what priests, pastors, and chaplains find in our hearts for those who confess.

"God forgives when we confess our sins. God waits until we are ready to bring Him into our pain."

She cries again, saying, "I have asked to be forgiven every time I hit her. I fear her verbal jabs at me. At times, these are more than I can bear and I'm not able to control myself. Now, I can't forgive myself for how many times I've slapped her face—even while hating myself for doing it."

"My dear lady, things will change now that you have told me this. Our staff here at the hospital will see to that. You will no longer be taking care of your mother."

"What will happen to her?" She is startled. Her elderly mother's care fell to her, as her mom has no money to provide for herself.

"I can assure you that this is beyond you, now. Experts will figure out what happens next. Your mother will be cared for. And, you will not be doing the care. I can promise you that."

I feel sadness for this woman, knowing the state steps in when elder abuse is involved. Here lies a safety issue that mandates reporting. Therefore, this patient's future remains to be seen, as elder abuse compels a legal judgment. I hope that judgment can be delivered with compassion. Still, my part of the hospital's teamwork is to tend to the patient's spiritual care. I encourage her to seek her pastor's help from here on. Priests, rabbis, pastors, and imams are part of the hospital team. Although not on the hospital's staff, all of them are important players in the work of helping and healing patients. Knowing this is comforting as a hospital chaplain. It is of vital importance that ongoing spiritual care be made available to this woman. She will soon leave the hospital and face whatever legal consequences that lie ahead, along with the emotional significance of abusing her mother.

"Would you like for me to read a passage of Scripture?" I ask.

"Yes. I would like that."

I turn to Isaiah 1:18-19. "Let me preface this passage with a bit from what happens just before God speaks these words to His children. To summarize, God was tired of watching sin continue within the ranks of His children. These were His chosen people. God had succored them and performed miracles among them. He had extended mercy over and over again while seeing their bad behavior. But they continued doing what they knew they should not do."

I am watching her face while talking, making sure she sees my compassion, not judgment. "God faces up to the children of Israel. He tells them that their behavior has to change. He then says something that may be very meaningful to you today. God says they are forgiven–fully cleansed–and will meet with blessing if only they will be obedient and have a change of heart. God leaves no doubt in their minds what He wants. He expects His people to follow the ways and the will of the Lord."

I pause, watching her demeanor. She is with me, soaking in what I'm saying. So I continue, "Now, listen to *these* beautiful words: 'Come now, let us reason together, though your sins are like scarlet, they shall be as white as snow, though they are red as crimson, they shall be like wool.' God is assuring His people that once forgiveness is given, the heart is cleansed. God does not hold past sins against us when we are truly sorry."

She looked at me with hope in her eyes. In the stillness of a long gaze, I sensed something was already taking place in her heart. I want her to take the lead. So, I wait.

"Would you please pray with me?" she asks.

"Certainly, I will. But, I would like you to start the prayer."

She is willing and I am moved while witnessing her fervent prayer for her heart to be cleansed "as white as snow." She also asks God for a change of heart toward her mother. I see a sincere outpouring of sorrow to God. I pray next, asking for this patient to begin the process of forgiving her mother for those difficult, early years—and for the healing of her mind, her spirit, and her body. Together we say The Lord's prayer. Afterwards, she adds, "Thank you, God. I feel such peace!"

I know this patient will be discharged soon. I have no idea what will take place for her once a social worker and I talk. It will be the social worker's job to report the abuse to the authorities. Then, the state will make sure continued care is provided for her mother. By the time this daughter is discharged, the team, here, will have a plan in place for the mother's ongoing care.

Working as a staff hospital chaplain means the next day's demands take priority over the previous day's challenges. I wish to know more about the future of this patient. Yet, part of a chaplain's job is to let go and move on. Back at the chapel, however, I had some emotions to work through and more prayers to say for these two women. Even to this day, I pray for each of them to be healed whenever the Holy Spirit brings them to mind.

Chapter Two

"God moves in a mysterious way
His wonders to perform."
(From William Cowper's hymn titled
"Light Shining Out of Darkness")

I was conflicted while listening to this patient. At first, there was sorrow in hearing about the ways in which she was abused early in her life. Then, as I learned about her striking her elderly mother numerous times, feelings of shock rose up. While pondering the words of this patient, I could not help thinking of my relationship with my dad. These thoughts bring up a lot of feelings, yet I zeroed in to be present to her. Her story shows "but for the grace of God," how my story could have ended.

The truth that my father and I did not do well with one another brings considerable sorrow. He was a good father in many ways. Regardless of that, we seemed unable to make a loving, bonding connection with one another. Years passed, then two younger siblings were born. I saw my father interacting differently with them in ways I longed to experience. His enjoyment of these new family members was impossible to miss. As a child, I could not understand why this was so. Jealousy was not a factor as I too loved and adored both my baby sister and later my brother, who came to us when I was thirteen.

As I look at the situation from a historical position, it brings a helpful insight. Life itself was very different--and difficult. This was during a time when World War II was terrifying, especially for parents. Celebrating the birth of a child, while their hearts were filled with fear, may not have been possible. That was when I was born. Six years later, at my sister's birth, the war was over and everyone was celebrating the news.

Reflecting back, I recall those moments. It was midday when I glance out the kitchen window in time to see a neighbor's car swing into our long driveway. No one gets out. I see the driver's head leaning outside the window as Mom walks up to see what the driver wants. There is not time for more than a sentence to be said between them before my mother starts jumping up and down. She is screaming. I run out the door as the neighbor's car pulls out of our driveway as quickly as he drove in. Tears are running down my mother's face. Finally, her words are clear, "The war is over!" She screams the same thing over and over again. "Billy will be home! Billy will be safe!" Seeing my mother's heart fling open with so much feeling is too much for me. I start to cry while realizing how much she feared never seeing her brother again.

At six years old, I had no knowledge of what it took to end the war. All I know, right then, is that my parents are the happiest I've ever seen them! They are smiling and laughing--saying things like, "the war is over!" And, "the world is safe again!" I hear talk about "no more rationing!" I have no idea what that means. Seeing them happy is enough for me.

Now, as an adult, I know a mammoth pressure was lifted from every living person. I believe, that made way for my parents to breathe more freely and bond with their younger children. Nonetheless, for me, an affectionate father-daughter relationship remained absent. As much as I tried to shake my sorrow over feeling "left out," it was felt impossible. At points, I invested effort toward initiating change in Dad's and my relationship, yet to no avail. Now, even after his death, I find those old feelings can still arise in a flash from deep in my subconscious mind. As these memories and feelings arise, begging for attention, my work is to let go of the sorrow, the disappointment, resentment, and my judgments of Dad. Fortunately, these "intruders" arise less and less often as I persist in releasing them.[3]

As I work with people, it seems grievances that happen to little children are often the most difficult to completely release. For this reason, the process of letting go and letting God heal the wounds from childhood does take time and effort. Through the process, we become overcomers.[4]

My childhood was lived mostly on a small farm, which was an adventure. Yet, we had times that were both wonderful and terrible. As a child, I was totally oblivious of the pressures my parents endured. I could not know what was causing their anguish, which at times came out sideways, resulting in needless punishments. I loved and admired my parents more than I feared them.

They were young, trying to earn a living on a postage-stamp farm of 40 acres. The Great Depression of the 1930s must have tied their emotions into a knot. Then, to have World War II follow hard on its heels created one of the most dreadful times in history. Many parents had children fighting every day on seas or foreign soil. My mother's brother, Bill, was on a battleship in the South Pacific. Mom feared his death, as ships were sunk by the enemy nearly every day. A great number of people living within that era were emotional wrecks. Others were barely able to cling to hope, as World War II caused immense worries. Fear wore on; no one knew whether the Japanese could take our country. Would Americans become prisoners of war? Or, would many be killed? These concerns must have torn through the soul of every adult during those years.

Today, while looking back, I am amazed Mom and Dad managed so well. They did a masterful job of keeping their fears of the war and financial struggles to themselves. This is something many parents fail to do, resulting in children carrying a stress they can do

---

[3] Addendum Page 117, titled "Inner Healing Exercise," offers a prayerful visualization that serves well when emotions do not release easily.

[4] There are several promises to "the overcomer" in the book of Revelation: Revelation 2:7, 2:11, 2:17, 2:26, 3:5, 3:12, 3:21 and 21:7.

nothing about. Anxiety disorders can develop early for a child who fears *"something bad is going to happen to me—and there is nothing I can do about it."*

I could not miss knowing my parents were troubled. A child tries to figure things out when they sense there are things to worry about. As for me, I thought my parents were mad at me. This prompted a sense of not being enough, or good enough. As an adult, I know that my parent's anger was about them, not about me. However, children are fully egocentric. They think everything has to do with them. That was me. Early on, *I thought everything was my fault.* Like all other adults at that time, my parents had no training in how best to discipline children. Even today, few parents are well prepared for parenting in a healthy way. This negatively impacts the lives of many people. Becoming an adult does not make all those hurtful memories melt away.

Although I did not comprehend my parents' hardships, certain other things influenced me indelibly. This is especially true in regards to the lack of emotional connectedness within our family. Given the uncertainty that existed in our home, it is easy to understand why I became overly responsible, perfectionistic, prone to feeling guilt, and unnecessarily ashamed.

What was great on the farm was having animals and playing games with neighboring friends. This allowed my joyful side to develop. Reading and studying also provided a great outlet. Dad gave money for every "A" on report cards; so I was motivated to love studying. That favorable attention was highly sought!

Life was never dull on the farm, although we were miles from town. Something was always happening and laughter often saved the day. So, now on occasions when our family of origin gets together, farm stories fly back and forth. One such story involves my father having to take jobs away from home, at times, in order to support the family. Neighbors helped one another during harvest time or when butchering took place. But, Dad met his waterloo when he needed to be away for a week while buying hay to sell. *Who would take care of the cows?* He wondered. The neighbors were all taking care of their own cows morning and night.

So, Dad propositioned Mom, "If you will milk the cows next week, I'll let you have the milk check." That money would come from a local creamery that picked up the milk at the end of the road every morning, seven days a week. At first she said, "No." Mom was raised in the city, but Dad taught her how to milk cows. She deplored this chore. She knew if she agreed to take on this task it would mean kneeling before those beasts twice a day. However, the idea of having extra money to spend was too much temptation for her. Mom agreed to do it.

Cows have a habit of swishing their tails to ward off bothersome flies. Being hit in the face by swishing tails, while trying to milk the cows, was getting to Mom. One morning, she dashed to the kitchen for scissors and then returned to the barn where she immediately cut all the hair off each cow's tail. Now she had a new problem. The next time she milked, Mom got hit with a switching tail that smacked her like a billy club.

When Dad came home and resumed the milking, he was upset over what those hard, hairless tails could do. After receiving a few clubbings, he was fuming! Dad's ingenuity kicked in. He rigged clamp-like holders from the ceiling of the barn and attached the cows' tails to these apparatus before milking. How funny the cows looked standing in their stanchions with their tails tied straight in the air while being milked! It seemed Dad would goad Mom forever about this tail business.

Mom had her turn at being mad when the milk check arrived. The check was for $1.38. They both had forgotten there was one more payment due on the cows the creamery had sold to them. That remaining payment of $100 came out of the milk check that belonged to Mom! For a week, Mom had milked those cows then pushed a cart carrying five 60-pound milk cans to the end of the road by 5:00 A.M.--all for $1.38!

The cows perpetually challenged Mom and Dad. They always had to be fed, milked, and medicated. And, they never paid their way.

No one could miss the fact Mom and Dad loved one another. In the evenings after dinner, while my older sister and I did the dishes, Mom and Dad would walk out into the fields at sunset with their arms around one another. That love between them was the greatest gift they could give to us as children. Their lives portrayed how love could be between a man and a woman. They were angry and afraid of the circumstances of their world. Yet, their anger was focused elsewhere, not on one another. They did disagree at times. A favorite memory is of Mom standing toe-to-toe with Dad while talking right into his eyes.

She said, "I want that unsightly scrap iron off the farm—or at least move it out of sight from the road."

Months passed. Nothing was moved. So Mom decided something needed to be done about this. She somehow managed to carry—and drag—several pieces of scrap iron to a nearby swamp. The dog and I stood on the canal bank watching her push and pull each piece until it dropped over the edge into the swamp. How fun it was witnessing that "junk" disappear!

Mom looked at me and said, "Don't you tell your father!"

Dad didn't notice for a long time. Then, one day I heard him say, "Josephine, the water in the swamp has receded. Would you like to tell me about what I found down there?" The way she looked at him said more than words. Mom never showed signs of being a pushover.

How many people can remember when they became conscious of sin? I can. That poignant moment happened a few weeks after one of my Dad's friends brought a barrel over and left it on our farm. I was curious and asked, "What's in it?" He said, "It's something terrible, too terrible to talk about. And, never cuss at it, or it will blow up!"

I had never cussed, but I had heard a lot of cussing at times when neighbors came to work with Dad at harvest time. I had to know if Freeman Cox, Dad's friend, was telling me the truth. So, upon getting up enough nerve, I picked out a tree about a hundred yards from the barrel, hid behind it, and cussed. Nothing happened. So, I got closer. Cussed again. Nothing. Finally, I walked up to the barrel, kicked it and cut loose with every bad word I had ever heard. Since the barrel didn't blow up, cussing at the barrel became my favorite pastime.

Mostly, this felt wonderful. It was as if I held power for the first time in my life. Later, at summer camp, I learned about Jesus and how He died for our sins. I immediately knew: Damn! I'm a sinner!

The unfortunate pattern of blocking my emotions—except for emoting at "my" barrel—could have prevailed. But, when I was eight years old, my Aunt Myrtle invited my parents to attend her church. It was a Pentecostal church, which included emotionality within worship. From that point on, Mom and Dad attended church with us kids in tow.

One of the first things they did was to start paying tithes. Well—if you want excitement—be poor and start paying tithes. At least, that is my take on it, because the revenue from the farm didn't change, it just stretched. Things happened one after another that kept us in awe. For instance, every car we ever owned was old. It took more hope than gas to run them. Then, came a huge sound from somewhere in the motor that blasted our ear drums and any thought of ever driving our car again. That left us calling on God! "What to do? We *have* to have a car!"

Three days later a man drove into our driveway in a highly polished "newish" Chevrolet. He stepped out, exchanged a few words with Dad, and then drove off again.

When Dad came back in the house he had a big smile on his face. "That man said he saw our corn cutter and wants to know if I will trade it for his car." I was in shock, waiting for Dad to say more. *The car! The car! We need the car* raced through my mind.

Finally, Dad said, "I don't need that corn cutter anymore—don't even use it now. But, I *do need that car*."

The car was glorious. "New," in our eyes—*and blue*, my favorite color! Many things began to change. Our neighbors were taking notice. Before long Mr. and Mrs. Black, who lived closest to us, started taking their family to church.

Now, going to church was my very favorite thing! At that early age, the presence of God was felt both in daily life and during church services. I remember amazing experiences within the congregation when we all felt God's presence at once. At these points, there came a "holy hush" for long moments. During praise and worship, my heart opened to God like an unfolding flower. While kneeling at the altar during prayer services, I began to reach and release my tears. Sometimes, these were tears of joy in sensing God's great love. Other times, my sorrow came up in sobs. These emotional releases undoubtedly influenced my ability to gradually feel life's pain, while also knowing God's love is great.

Consequently, my parents found themselves on a path that eventually saw them ministering in several foreign countries. My father prayed for sick people and some were healed. However, it was different for me. At age 13, chronic appendicitis presented frequent pain. Dad prayed for me over and over again. I got worse instead of better. When my doctor insisted on surgery, Dad decided that I was doing something wrong or that I did not have enough faith. "Otherwise, you would be healed," he said. At that moment, what could have helped me most would have been to have my father put his arms around me and say, "I love you. We will get through this together." Unfortunately, that did not happen. Some people cannot express a full range of emotions, and that was true of my Dad.

Finally, an appendectomy was performed. I was dreadfully ashamed, though, as Dad and Mom still believed my faith had fallen short. The guilt I felt stayed with me, whereas the appendicitis was healed through the hands of a surgeon. I felt like a failure over disappointing Mom and Dad.

Months after having an appendectomy, I experienced my legs going stiff while walking in the hall at school. I fell to the floor and could not get up. My parents were called. Kids were everywhere–gawking! It seemed like forever before Mom and

Dad arrived to take me home. I had to be carried. During the next two weeks, I read a book by Tommy Tyson on healing. After finishing it, I prayed to be healed—and immediately I could move my legs, again. They were completely normal! What a marvelous healing! The doctor soon verified that I no longer had the rare, crippling condition he had diagnosed. Our whole family was excited about this healing of mine. Now, I was sure healings can happen, even for me.

At age 13, I also came close to death from encephalitis, an inflammation of the brain that caused fevers reaching 106 degrees. The fevers fluctuated and lasted for weeks. Although encephalitis often kills a person, I amazed everyone by getting well!

The doctor was happy, but puzzled. He told my mother, "There should have been massive brain damage." He called it "a miracle," then said, "A high, intense fever of such a long duration should have completely burned through Joy's brain, leaving her with grave disability."

Again, I experienced a healing. God answered the many prayers of my family and the members of our church. God protected my brain! So now, I wondered why God healed me two different times, but not when I needed healing for appendicitis? With both illnesses, the same people were interceding in prayer for me, asking for my healing. Of course, I was praying as well, believing the Lord would heal me.

The message from my father that I did not have enough faith to be healed heavily influenced my self-worth. It even affected my sense of what God is like, what God wanted of me. I loved God, yet feared Him. Within the church of my childhood, people were ministered to for the purpose of healing through the laying on of hands with prayer. Our pastor never taught that healing was dependent on the individual having enough faith. At *church*, the ministry of healing was carried out with care and compassion. Dad's beliefs came from his own interpretation of the Scriptures. He was blindsided when it came to me. He did not realize how hurtful his words were and how they created a trap of guilt in me that sprung quickly and easily.

As mentioned in Chapter One, I had episodes of traveling blood clots. At age eighteen, I had my first pulmonary emboli in which bloods clot entered my lungs).

The doctor said, "This is like living on a stick of dynamite. You will never know when it is going to blow." He treated me with blood thinning medication each time a blood clot traveled to my heart, then landed in my lungs. It was puzzling as to why this kept happening. A hematologist did every possible study of my blood that was available to him at that time. When no cause could be found, he determined this condition was my body's way of dealing with stress.

Many people don't live through blood clots shooting through their heart and then into their lungs! Pulmonary emboli often kill within a first episode. I credit the fact of my survival to the prayers of others, along with my trust in God's mercy and power to keep me alive.

While doing my inner work I could not help but ponder Mary Shelley's novel, *Frankenstein*, and how her stories are called "blood curdling." That adage of something being fearsome enough to curdle one's blood has been around for a very long time. It is not hard to think of blood clots having some roots from childhood, as there was a lot going on in our household that was scary to me. Locking down on the emotions of fear, shame, sadness, and anger perhaps served to tie my soul in knots. My body may have portrayed that through blood clots. Knowing this potential gives every reason for diligently identifying and working through difficult emotions. I was also determined to continue working to forgive everyone and every event in life that hurt or harmed me. Resentment, grudges, and even disappointments had to be taken to God. It would take time, but eventually these would hold no power over me. The difficulties of the past definitely marked my life. But, God is the Great Recycler. He recycled all that happened, replacing them with forgiveness, mercy, and compassion. How wonderful of God!

My father suffered the last weeks of his life with esophageal cancer. I traveled to be with him as often as I could, always hoping that as the end of his life grew near he and I could somehow build a bridge onto which we could step and reach out to one another. I wanted so much to have closeness with Dad before he died. However, when I spoke of loving him he maintained silence.

I dreamed of Dad and I talking openly about life's struggles and life's joy, but that did not happen between us. I could only hope Dad would talk to me during those last years as he faced various physical ailments. I could not help but wonder: *Would he remember what he said to me all those times about me not having enough faith to be healed?* I was never tempted to bring it up. Doing so would surely hurt him. I imagined talking about what went wrong between us. If only we *could talk*! Then, we could hug and maybe have some tears together. Perhaps we could even laugh about ourselves and what kept us from one another all those years. Maybe it was his male pride behind the silence, but I longed for him to share his heart with me. Then, during one of my last visits with Dad, who was now 95 and in assisted living, I found the courage to ask, "Dad, could I pray for you?" Dad was always *"the pray-er"* when it came to the laying on of hands and praying for another. So, I knew he might be put off with me for asking. I was relieved when he paused, then said, "Yes."

I used anointing oil given to me by a priest back in my days within the Roman Catholic community. Tracing the sign of the cross on his forehead, I said, "Dad, I anoint you with this oil as a sign of our belief in Christ's healing power." He was silent, seeming to OK my prayer. He was dying; his cancer was advanced.

Although I did not pray for a physical healing, I did have the faith to pray for my father to feel very much loved. I asked God many times throughout his last months of life to fill my father's being with the knowledge of my love. Yet, I had no sign of that happening. At his funeral, I wept so hard my body was racked with pain. It was clear to me that I was grieving over believing my father never knew me as a daughter whom he could enjoy and love. The two of us were so much alike in our love of God and our love of studies. Yet, we were somehow unable to enjoy that alikeness.

Dad's memory is loved and treasured by many. What is helping my soul, presently, is to not fight the feelings that sometimes come up as regards my father. These are out of my control. The part of my psyche that consists of my subconscious mind is still working to make sure all the past is adequately dealt with. I'm not failing to forgive when the feelings come up. So, there is no guilt involved. Each time, though, I have to release each and every difficult feeling to God. It is a choice I continue to make. One I will not go back on.

Instead of being a victim, *I choose to be an overcomer*! Now, I feel free to continue to send love to both my mother and my father, hoping this love somehow reaches them in heaven. If not, this prayer form helps me continue to heal. God's work in me is the fulcrum from which I give grace and mercy to my father. I am now able to forgive his inabilities, knowing full well I have my own incompleteness.

Our mistakes are different, yet I am no more perfect than my parents. Fortunately, for each of us, we are forgiven–covered by God's grace. When we need to forgive something or someone, it can take time. Actually, some events take a lifetime of work as old, painful memories keep coming up, reminding us of what happened "back when." Working and reworking the process takes patience and humility–fruits of the Holy Spirit into which God calls us to grow.

A book titled *Fearfully and Wonderfully Made,*[5] by Dr. Paul Brand and Philip Yancey, skillfully portrays how, along with our bodies being awesomely made, our souls are also wonderfully put together through everything we learn and experience along life's road. Given time and a desire to follow the teachings of Christ, we become who God wants us to be in spite of difficulties, losses, limitations, and failures. Through increments, we are woven into the persons we are intended to become. It is a process through which God uses every experience of our lives, both good and bad, to form and shape us for being His people on the earth. Through us, His plan for the world unfolds. Can there be any doubt that

---

[5] Paul Brand and Phillip Yancey, *Fearfully and Wonderfully Made – A Surgeon Looks at the Human & Spiritual Body* (Michigan: Zondervan, 1965).

The Chaplain is in: Journey to Health and Happiness

His plan is hinged on forgiveness?

Joy Le Page Smith

Pastoral Incident # 3

As I enter the room, Katie[6] is sleeping. Her sister crosses the room and whispers, "Chaplain, I'm very worried about my sister. I can't explain what she is so upset about. She is sleeping lightly and probably will wake up soon. Would you please try to help her?"

As she leaves the room, I answer, "Yes, I will be glad to talk with her." I sit in a chair beside Katie and pray silently, "Lord, I don't know what the problem is here, but you do. Please give me an opportunity to talk with this patient. If she will talk with me, please help me know what *You* would say to her."

Before long, a nurse walks in with medication, waking Katie.

The nurse is finished. She leaves and I introduce myself, "I'm Chaplain Joy. I am making rounds with patients and wonder if you feel up to talking a bit?"

She thinks for a moment, and says, "Yes, I would like that." Then, as quick as a wink, she asks two questions as an afterthought: "Are you a Bible-believing Christian? Are you saved?"

These questions don't surprise me. She wants to know if she can trust this stranger who calls herself a chaplain.

"May I call you Katie?"

"Sure."

"Yes, I am a Christian. My trust is in Jesus Christ, as my Lord and Savior."

Katie seems to relax a bit, and then begins, "I can't believe in prayer anymore, Chaplain. And, I'm very miserable. I believe in God. But I'm not getting well–in fact, I may die!" She clutches at

---

[6] When names or initials are used within this book these have been changed to protect the privacy of individuals. Circumstances are also changed, within this writing, to assure individuals are not identified.

the sheet; I see how white her skin is.

Katie continues, "My doctor keeps doing tests and is making it clear that my condition is serious. I've prayed for many months now, believing God will heal me. The elders of my church came to my home and prayed, anointing me with oil three months ago. They say God heals if we pray and receive it. They left me with a list of Scriptures on the subject of healing. I read each one of them. I have believed–and I've prayed to be healed more times than I can count. Still, my blood work shows no change. The disease I have is rare…and I'm getting sicker! *I'm not getting well!*"

I see disappointment in her face. I respond, "Katie, I'm sorry you are ill. And I'm sorry you are feeling troubled over what seems like unanswered prayer. Could I tell you my own story?"

"Yes."

I continue, "Something very similar to your situation happened to me, Katie. About twenty years ago, I was a young mother, in the hospital, knowing that I was close to death. Yet, I needed, *ever so much*, to live. I wanted to finish raising my three children. Like you, I was taught to believe that divine healing comes through prayer and the laying-on-of-hands. When I didn't get healed, after many times of being prayed over, I was told, 'You don't have enough faith. That's why you are not healed.' I followed the directives of well-intended people at my church. I remember feeling strange when one of our elders said to me, 'Ask the Lord to help you *see* if there is sin in your life that has not been confessed.' He meant well; yet I felt bad. I was already feeling a lot of shame, since the many prayers for healing seemed to go unheard. Some anger began to build."

I can see by her demeanor that Katie and I are making a connection. I tell her my history of enduring hospital stays, after multiple blood clots shooting through my heart, then into my lungs.

"Katie, I too lamented my poor health." Her eyes well-up with tears as I mention my three young sons and my fear of dying, leaving them without a mother. *They are men, now,* Katie, raising their own families. *I am a grandmother!"* I say with a huge smile. In my heart, I thank God again for my own wellness, as I sit there before this patient.

I take the time, now, to explain my own struggles while leading up to a truth which I think will encourage her. "Katie, my healing came with time. Medical doctors did their part in keeping me alive, and then the Lord took over, healing me in a way that continues to mystify others. She smiles as I add, "Mind you, I was *too sick to muster more faith*–but it happened anyway!"

Katie is particularly interested in hearing more about the unique way God helped me get well. I continue, "For one thing, I learned that God works differently with each person who seeks to be healed."

Her eyes dance a bit when I add, "God doesn't have *a healing thermometer* gauging the amount of faith you or I have."

Sometimes, while with patients, silence allows truth to sink in. I wait ...then say, "Katie, ask God to help you forgive the hurt that comes to you at this time. He cares. My experience tells me that God helps us when we determine to forgive those who have hurt us throughout life. There is a powerful inner healing taking place when we forgive. I've read medical studies that verify this.

She is very quiet. Then, her eyes search my face as if to ask, *is all this true?* I pray inwardly, "Lord, help Katie receive what it is that You have for her today."

I notice the clock. I feel an inner nudge that seems to affirm my need to *ignore the time, stay put.* The next patient can wait. I sense God is not done here. So I add, "Katie, God's timing and God's way of healing is always the best. Can you trust that?"

"Yes. I want to trust that."

Her whole being seems to grow lighter as I speak of being led to train as a chaplain, once I was well. I tell her of the joy I find in this work that allows me to use all my life experiences for the purpose of bringing God's help to those who hurt.

"Katie, God is at work in us. There is not a pat formula for reaching healing. And, as hard as this is to hear, death is the ultimate healing for a believer."

There is pain in her eyes as Katie speaks of her children and her fear that she may not live long enough to raise them. She tells of her great desire to finish her education as a nurse. Her tears are different, now. She has taken my hand. I see a gentle joy come over her face. It seems she knows I am living proof that there is hope.

"Katie, I cannot know what your tomorrow holds. But what I do know is that you are not suffering alone. God is with you. I also know this: when we don't get what we want—what we have prayed for and longed after—believing God should give it to us, there is a real likelihood God has something better for us."

Her mood changes. I sense her strength arising and hope growing. She says, "I believe in God, *for sure*. I just can't believe in myself...I can't believe I am worthy of God's loving care."

"No one is any more worthy than you are, Katie. God's mercy sets aside the sins of each of us and covers it *forever* with love. This is true regardless of anything you or I have done that we wish we had not done. It is true for every living person. And, when we love the Lord, our lives are full of confessing, including our confessions of love and gratitude, praise and thanksgiving."

She smiles and falls silent for two or three minutes, then says gently, "I'd like to believe God is not mad at me or disappointed in me."

"Katie, this thing of being a Christian is about relationship. It is about trusting in God's loving acceptance—knowing that the love of God is beyond anything we humans can comprehend. *Above all*, Katie, you are loved!"

"But, what about God being angry?" She says. "In the Old

Testament I read of God being angry—a lot—over the sins and failures of His people."

My answer comes from many years of living. I say, "The truth I rely on, Katie, is that Jesus brought us a whole new revelation of God. In reading the New Testament, you will see the face of God. And, you will see the loving heart of God in Jesus. You will know that God's will for you is laid out within the Lord's teachings. The Holy Spirit will help you comprehend the love of God, more than ever. Pray, asking God to help you trust in the love of God as you read the Scriptures. Put aside all that others have said about Jesus' life and Jesus' words. Read the Gospels, prayerfully, while listening for God's truth *to you* within each time of reading. In this way, the Holy Spirit will help you hear what God has for you each day."

"Would you pray for me?" Katie asks.

"Sure," I say. "You start and I will finish, okay?"

Katie's prayer needs nothing to be added by me. It is one of the most beautiful prayers of love and humility that I've heard. I add a prayer of blessing for her, asking God to comfort her within the illness she is enduring. Holding her hand, I wait, knowing again that it is not time to leave. It only takes five or so minutes before she is asleep. I carefully disengage our entwined fingers.

Chapter Three

*"Deep joy is both the ground of love
and the surest source of strength to persevere
...even when trials abound, as they often will."*
Robert Ellwood

Strange as this may seem, I "had to forgive God." In truth, that statement is the poorest of all theology. Still, it is where some of us are until we get a grip on what is really true. My problem was based in projecting my earthly father onto God. Consequently, I knew Jesus as my Lord, but for a very long time I drew a blank when attempting to comprehend God as "Father." I saw Him as Creator of my soul and was always exceedingly grateful to *this God* that I could accept. I just didn't call Him "Father."

Later, in my work as a chaplain, I encounter many women who do not do well with God because of having fathers they have trouble forgiving. From my experience of feeling left out and overpowered by my father, it is easy for me to understand their struggles. For some, it is nearly impossible to relate with God. They are blocked from seeing God as a father who is interested in them, let alone compassionate. It hurts to hear their stories. What happened to many of them, within their father relationships, was far-and-wide more troublesome than what I experienced with my father. Yet, suffering is suffering. It never helps to compare our own sufferings with those of others. Meanwhile, it never ceases to amaze me how all in life can shape us and make us more able to support and benefit others.

A Father God healing took place for me when I attended an eight-day silent retreat at the Nazareth Retreat Center.[7] As it happened, deciding to set this time aside to be with God instigated an astounding experience. We were nearing the end of the retreat when Bishop Trienen, of the Boise Diocese, directed participants to read Scripture passages portraying the trial and crucifixion of Jesus. He said, "Allow yourselves to enter into that experience as fully as possible. In doing so, you can better comprehend God's gift to us through Christ Jesus." He prays that the Lord's passion and death would reach our souls as never before.

I go to my room hoping the Scriptures will come alive for me, yet not knowing how powerfully that could happen. A crucifix hangs on the wall; it seems to beckon my touch. I grab some pillows for propping, take the crucifix off-the-wall, and sit on the floor. I slowly read while pondering the assigned passages, then close the Bible. I say, "Lord, here I am." It hurt to give my full attention to each step of His suffering. Then, while expressing my love for Him, an astounding happening takes hold of me. I am transported as if "in the Spirit" to Golgotha where Jesus is crucified. Suddenly, I am watching everything that takes place there. What a grievous experience! I cry aloud and am anguished, watching the soldiers pound huge spikes through Jesus' flesh. I see the blood running from his head, hands, and feet. As I weep, a fervent plea escapes my lips, "*Why* did you let them do this to you?"

Jesus looks at me with *such eyes*—eyes that speak of infinite love...*eyes that penetrated my soul*. He says, "So that *you* might be free."

It felt as if my heart would break. I *knew* I was *not* free. It made no sense to me, vividly seeing Him there, nailed on that wretched wooden cross. I recalled His words to me. But, all I could think was *if He died for me to be free, He failed to accomplish what He*

---

[7] Nazareth Retreat Center is within the Boise Diocese of the Roman Catholic Church in Idaho.

set out to do! I had been a Christian since age eight—and I still had plenty of emotional baggage to battle on a daily basis. *Free? Not me!*

Then, in an instant, I am allowed to feel the wondrous freedom that he intended. It is not possible to describe how great that joy is*! It is incredible*—lasting long moments. I laugh in response to such an astonishing *joy*. At last I know what it feels like for my soul to be completely *free*. But, that sense of freedom leaves as quickly as it comes, plunging me into the truth: that freedom is not present in my life. Acknowledging this, my emotions instantly change to the opposite of joy. A great sorrow comes over me. Jesus died so I can be *free*—and my truth is far too clear. I am *not free!* Then another emotional switch—into the tremendous joy felt earlier! My emotions flip like this, over and over again. Only God knows how much time is involved. First, the joy comes, and then the sorrow—back and forth. I am totally captured in the experience of seeing how very different these two places-of-being truly are.

I knew Jesus provided the joy that came during those moments. And, I knew my day-by-day experiences did not include such a profound joy as the Lord is letting me see and experience. *He told me He died for this*! He doesn't want me to carry sins, failures, and abusive memories. He died to carry these! I am meant to be *free* of all this!

For an hour each day during the retreat, participants met with an appointed spiritual director. My vision is still powerfully affecting my emotions, but I gather myself up off the pillows to meet with Fr. John Donoghue. Sitting across from him in his office, I open my mouth, but cannot speak. I want to tell him what happened, but start crying instead. Then, I laugh as I feel that *joy* rolling inside me, again! He watches and listens. Finally, I can tell Fr. John of my vision.

He ponders, as if to think carefully, and then says, "You have had a great consolation. I don't know what God is doing through this experience. But, you will find out. Trust the Father. He will make it clear to you."

Yikes! This "Father" word triggered a bit of a "ka-pow!" I have passed over the "Our Father" part of the Lord's Prayer throughout the years. I don't want to revive the pain of feeling shunned by my father. Now, I prayed to garner all the truth I could from the vision I am given. There is no doubt the vision is a privilege and the Holy Spirit is getting a message across: "It is your Father God who is allowing this vision. He wants your attention." Well, He has it, now!

Being called to the higher ground of going deeper into relationship with not just Jesus and the Holy Spirit, but with *the Father* is superb and profound! From there on, I began toying with the thought *God is my father*. Father God is the One who called me into being—and it is my Father God who has always been with me through Christ! I saw how it was God hanging on that cross in the body and soul of Jesus. It was not easy to get my head around all of this. It took time and contemplation to absorb it.

Proverbs 29:18 assures us of a truth we don't want to miss: where there is *no vision*, the people perish. There is a certain "perishing" that takes place on a daily basis when emotional struggles gain a stranglehold, robbing us, God's children, of the peace and the joy which is our intended heritage. In certain ways, I was "perishing" for lack of understanding that God *The Father* wanted my love.

I eventually reached an insight that was freeing: My dad's great desire was always for me to get well. That was the purpose for his practicing the laying-on-of-hands with prayers for my healing. It has taken time to see past what those experiences were like for me and to gain a fuller understanding. Dad's gift was new to him and he thought everybody would get healed *if they had enough faith*. He apparently thought I could muster up more faith. Meanwhile, I could only see the struggle of feeling bad about him and super-bad about myself.

Through the years, I knew as a Christian I should forgive my father. So I told God, "I forgive him." Then Dad would, again, insist on praying for me. The cycle of being hurt, angry and afraid continued. My fear had to do with the "what ifs." What if he was right? What if I could never please God ...and that nothing I did was ever *good enough*? The psyche picks up old songs and sings them over and over. Within my ongoing desire to stop feeling bad toward my father, it became clear to me that forgiving is a process. In the midst of realizing Dad's prayers were alienating me, I had to *persist* in letting go those feelings that kept coming up. Freedom would come through reminding myself, *I have set my will to forgive him.* The Lord addressed this with Peter when he asked, "Lord, how often shall my brother sin against me, and I forgive him? Up to seven times? Jesus said to him, 'I do not say to you, up to seven times, but up to seventy times seven'" (Mt 18:21-22). It was comforting to believe God only expected of me what I could do at the time.

Isn't it strange that truth comes so slowly, until God helps us by making things crystal clear? My father had no way of knowing his words, "You do not have enough faith to be healed," rang in my head long after he spoke them. He did not know my physical pain was worsened by the shame that resulted for me. I didn't tell him. The two of us could not communicate. What stopped me from saying, "Dad, I am getting a double whammy, here?" It was my deeply instilled fear of him. And, there were ways in which I projected that fear onto God. I began to see how that, at least in part, affected my trust in God.

The day came when I realized judging my father was keeping me stuck. And, I saw the difference between sorrowing over loss and wallowing in self-pity and judgment of my father. I learned that, yes, it is important to grieve what is painful in life while also watching for times when self-pity comes out to play. It was through that event of bawling and shouting at God about my predicament, without holding back, that I discovered God accepts me just as I am. I was coming to the truth that, as fallible human beings, our identity is *in Christ*. *It is the Lord* who is doing the work of healing as we surmount failures and mistakes, past and present. It greatly improves a person's self-esteem to know that "warts and all" we are God's beloved adult children who are *making progress*.

I had to get real with God about what was hidden inside my psyche under a pile of self-centeredness, low self-esteem, and self-pity. Honesty with God came one day, right in the middle of my living room. It was not a pretty scene, as anger and forceful crying went on for some time. I shouted at God, "This isn't working! *Enough of this!*"

I blamed God for my having all those brushes with death. *What was He thinking!* Of course, I was working with half-baked theology. Now, God was getting the brunt of this mammoth load of pent up emotions!

I felt justified in my claim, "God, no one in my family is sick! Just me! You gave my father a healing ministry—and a lot of people think he is great! Why is it that when he prays over others *they get healed, and I don't?*"

"God, You equipped Dad with a powerful gift, then you make sure it doesn't work on me? You have seen all those times when he laid hands on me and prayed for my healing! Well, what about me?" Now, my "father-grudge" was plastered onto God and pouring out fervently. It was not pretty.

After walking, ranting, and emoting with full force, I sit down. All that forceful wind is out of my sails. So, I asked, "God, what do you think of me *now*?"

I hear back, "I knew it was there all along." A sense of being loved and accepted follows in the midst of all those words and emotions. I know God wanted me to blow all that father-sludge out of my system—with handkerchief in hand.

Although I couldn't know it early on, I was given *the father* that would best serve God's overall plan and purpose for me. Because of who Dad was with his limitations—and who I was with mine—we both had lots of grist for our spiritual mills.

I had my times of slipping into self-pity—and wanting to escape daily pain. One night, as I lie in my bed unable to sleep, pain was, again, bringing me close to the end of my endurance. Many feelings were crowding in. The "why me" question rode the wave of pity. Poor me. On the wall facing the foot of my bed the closet door stood open. In this closet there were several bottles of whiskey, standing there like dusty soldiers. These belonged to Gary, as they were gifts from his employer during several past Christmases. None of them were open, as Gary did not drink hard liquor. He kept them, saying, "Someday these will age and be valuable." But that night I lay in my bed thinking of their value differently. I knew they held potential to end this pain. My next thought was one of fear. I had several uncles who were alcoholics. Being a teetotaler brought a sense of safety. Gary was working the late night shift at Greyhound, but I knew it was time to call him. My head is pounding by the time he answers.

"Gary, when you get home tonight I need you to dump out each of those bottles of whiskey in the closet."

He said, "Why should I do that?"

"Because if I open one and start to drink, I'm afraid I'll never stop."

"Then *you* dump them yourself. Right now," Gary says.

So, I climb up in the closet. One-by-one I hug each bottle to my chest before taking them to the kitchen sink. It is an astounding time. I am numb as I hear the "gluck, gluck, gluck" of the fluid, while watching its golden power flow down the drain. There is no laughter in this. Yet, this is the cure I need for the fear caused by knowing I might start drinking that liquor.

Both self-pity and alcoholism waved flags of temptation during the years while my illness was so persistent. Only through God's help in my life could I resist these. I had a choice. I could keep taking my pain to God, letting Him grow me spiritually, enabling me to rise above my circumstance–or I could stay stuck in self-willfulness and self-pity. I found the latter was not where I wanted to pitch my tent!

Karl Rahner, one of my favorite theologians, explained there are "layers of freedom" that come to us as we seek God wholeheartedly. To the degree we press forward, longing to grow in the truth of God and what His intention is for us, our freedom increases. Again, I hear Jesus saying, "you shall know the truth, and the truth shall make you free" (Jn 8:32).

In time, I realized that it was my family of origin, in which I was placed, that created a huge thirst for gaining more and more knowledge and experience of God. It was getting easier to trust that God is at work in *everything that happens* in my life.

I could not forget the freedom and the joy felt during the experience I had at the Nazareth Retreat Center. In the years to come, I read the Bible with greater fervor and began to study psychology while attending many workshops, retreats, and lectures in hopes of truly capturing the truth that would set me free. Since it was there to be had–I wanted it! My journey to joy was *achieved step-by-step*. It was through the adventures of those workshops, retreats, lectures, and biblical Scriptures that unlocked the door to *the joy and freedom* I longed for! And, this joy truly is "the ground of love and the surest source of strength," as Robert Ellwood stated.

Once, at a conference in Scottsdale I met Bruce H. Lipton, Ph.D., a guest speaker. Dr. Lipton is a leading edge scientist in cellular biology and author of *The Biology of Belief*.[8] Dr. Lipton described his research about how cells receive information. "A major breakthrough came," He said, "through learning that our cells respond to what we are thinking. Therefore, our bodies react favorably with every positive thought we have." In view of this, think of how our bodies can benefit when we *rejoice in the Lord, offering gratitude to God* for the gift of life and for all the provisions we are granted. Imagine, how good it must be for our cells when we ponder *God's goodness*! While listening to Dr. Lipton, I felt enthused, once again, about the power we have toward improving and safeguarding our health.

Paul Tournier, a Swiss physician for nearly fifty years, became known for his unique style of working with people. His practice was in the early to mid-twentieth century. He had no special training as a psychiatrist or psychologist. Still, it is said of him that few psychiatrists have helped as many patients solve their

---

[8] Bruce H. Lipton, *The Biology of Belief* (California: Hay House, Inc., 2011).

problems as this medical doctor. Why? Because he discovered what he called the "medicine of the person," in which Tournier combined his medical knowledge and expertise, with spirituality.

In *The Adventure of Living*, Tournier writes about an instinct peculiar to human beings, which he sees as the great impulse toward adventure. A dictionary definition of the word "adventure" is "an unusual experience or course of events marked by excitement and suspense." The premise Tournier extends here is that our "tremendous need for adventure, which is always ready to break out, takes countless forms." Tournier says we are wired with the need to solve mysteries and resolve challenges. An adventure begins when a problem or situation begs for a solution. In his last analysis, Tournier said that underneath all the various personal adventures "is an expression of man's hunger and thirst after God."[9]

Seeking intimate rapport with the Lord Jesus Christ changes everything for us. He teaches us to have the faith of a little child. This does not mean we are to hold onto childish patterns. Instead, we are meant to grow in our understanding and in our capacity to love and forgive. Forgiveness is letting go of the emotional and mental resistance that stands in the way of releasing the people who have hurt us—as well as to release our own bad decisions. This way, our resentment and grudges toward others, along with what we hold against ourselves, can respond. They will ebb away as we persist in setting our wills to be free of these impediments. Otherwise, when we hang onto resentments, saying, "I'm not ready to let them go! He [or she] hurt me too much—and doesn't deserve my forgiveness!" we are fooling ourselves.

For sure, that other person is not suffering from what you or I are thinking and feeling. We, on the other hand, are giving away our time and energy! All because we think that hanging onto judgments or resentments serves some purpose!

---

[9] Paul Tournier, *The Adventure of Living,* trans. Edwin Hudson (New York: Harper & Row, 1965).

One popular teacher points out that each day we are given a new supply of energy. We have 100% renewed supply every morning upon awakening. She claims that for each person we have not forgiven, we lose 30 percent of our energy. That is a huge amount of energy to lose every day. This is hard to comprehend. Yet, if it is less, like 10 percent, even that is a tremendous loss with each person we fail to forgive. Think of what this means if there are three people we can't forgive. Who among us wants to give up 30 percent of our daily energy? Whatever the percentage, a huge toll comes with carrying around judgments, anger, resentment, or ill will toward others, *or ourselves*, because of something from the past. These are not burdens Jesus wants us to carry.

Another trap comes in thinking that holding onto a grudge wises us up and somehow protects us from being hurt again. The fact remains that failure to forgive will pull us down and affect the essence of who we are. Conversely, having *the faith of a child* finds us trusting "Father knows best." We cannot read Scripture on a daily basis without knowing God has our best interests in mind. And, the Lord asks us to forgive. Sometimes that is hard to do. But, we can do hard things!

In Matthew 11:30, Jesus refers to His "yoke" and how it is easy to bear. The word "yoke" may seem to represent a burden, but when all is factored in, the yoke of Christ's teachings makes life easy and light, compared to going it alone without the comfort and guidance of the Holy Spirit. That yoke is truth. And, *it is true* that–even though it is a hard thing to do–we must forgive if we want life to go easier for us physically, mentally, and spiritually. Perhaps deep down, we know this. Yet, we need to keep telling ourselves the truth *until we live it*!

Forgiveness is without a doubt the fulcrum of Christianity. I have met people who think God will overlook it when they deem it impossible to forgive a wrong. Clearly, that is a fallacy. Forgiving a person may take time, but persistently working the process is urgently important. There is a serious problem in our theology if we think we can skip the part of Christ's teachings that involves forgiving everyone who has brought harm to us. It is also true, that forgiving does not mean we put up with bad behavior.

Remaining friends with a person, tolerating their unacceptable actions, is not part and parcel to forgiving them.

This truth causes me to smile. If we persist in holding something against another, it doesn't hurt them—not even a smidgen. On the other hand, letting that person keep on hurting us while nothing is felt on their end is poor self-care. Good self-care is important for healthy living. And, good self-care means we have good boundaries within relationships. [10]

It is not hard to see clearly that our Lord wants us to forgive. What *is hard* is doing it. At points, this necessitates doing some inner healing work. This sees us looking at our motives, attitudes, and intentions. Then, with the Lord's help, we grow in our ability to *see* what is going on within ourselves. *Seeing* what needs healing is 50 percent of the battle. Changing habits, patterns, and motives is the other 50 percent of the work. God always helps us reach our goals, when we earnestly press forward—and preserver. Success comes as we persist.

The medical field of psychoneuroimmunology shows the act of forgiving as holding amazing benefits. Ultimately, letting go of what we are holding against ourselves—and forgiving others—are two of the most powerful things we can do as regards our physical, emotional, and mental health. As Christians we trust in God's forgiveness. Taking the step of forgiving ourselves, however, presents a different element of the work. It is challenging for some of us. Yet, carrying this to the point of success is imperative. Why? Because God loves us and wants us to be whole. We cannot be whole if we are holding things against ourselves, or others. Above all, God desires our wellbeing and knows that failing to forgive will, without a doubt, bite us on the posterior side—if not in a vital organ. As for me, it took a lot of time to "real-ize" the breadth and width of making forgiveness a continual practice.

---

[10] Setting boundaries within relationships is essential for good self-care. For more help on this topic visit my website at www.healing-with-Joy.com (Click on the "Quick Aids" link for "Setting Boundaries Within Relationships.")

My response to the father-relationship given to me has become one of praise and thanksgiving. I have found God as a trustworthy, loving Father, who walks and talks with me in this spiritual relationship we now have. It brings me joy knowing I am done with blaming my father and blaming God; yet, my journey always includes watching for other childish beliefs and attitudes that may crop up.

The level of freedom I've come to enjoy in the Lord is greatly enhanced by accepting the truth that everything difficult in my life's adventure brings me closer to total dependence on God, while relying on the teachings of Christ.

Think of this: It was because the people in authority refused to recognize Jesus' ministry that He was pressed to the max. Rising above it all, He went to the cross. There, while His life ebbed away, Jesus said, "Father, forgive them. For they do not know what they do" (Luke 23:34). Surely, that forgiveness provided by Christ is the greatest of all gifts in our lives. He has brought us the Father, who loves and welcomes the prodigal that lies within us all. This is the Father who is perfect and dependable *in all ways*–ever ready to listen to us and recognize us as His very own beloved children.

The Chaplain is in: Journey to Health and Happiness

Pastoral Incident # 4

Note: I share the following as an example of how all of us help others during unexpected moments. In this instance, the knowledge extended is not commonly known. After reading this Pastoral Incident and Chapter Four, readers may have a greater understanding for a condition few can comprehend. This information can easily make a difference in the lives of desperate people. God alone will lead by the Holy Spirit as to how this newly gained information can augment another's journey. I am convinced that each of us can do the work of a chaplain at given times, within situations wherein our hearts are touched and we know immediately what it is we are to do or to say.

I am in the dentist office waiting for my appointment. As usual, I bring a book to read. However, the loud voice of a teenager tears into my concentration.

Speaking to her mother, the girl says, "I will not go in there! And you can't make me!" I think her age is about 17.

Her mother replies, "You have to. You have a broken tooth. It has to be taken care of."

The girl raises her voice and begins berating her mother. She ends with, "And, you *cannot* make me do this!" Everything about this mother indicates class and culture. I watch as she remains in control of herself; yet, the look on her face speaks of her inner angst and uncertainty. She tells her daughter to sit tight for a minute while she uses the restroom. Having raised three sons, I know she is giving herself a few moments of time out.

While this woman collects herself in the restroom I wonder if her daughter will stay. Soon I hear her loudly whispering and laughing to herself as if she is interacting with another person. In a flash, I realize I am looking at a scenario that I know so well. I am seeing afresh the realities of a very close friend whose daughter is also a teen with mental illness. My first thoughts go to similarities in the two situations. My heart is touched as I know this young woman before me has a long and difficult road ahead of her, as does her mother. I say inwardly, *Oh, no, God! She is so beautiful and strong. I'm sure this mother holds great hopes for her life*! Yet, I know the losses she faces and how her family will mourn.

Her mother returns and sits beside her daughter. Within a moment or two the dentist's assistant calls her into the exam room. Fortunately, the girl goes in. Now, the mother and I are the only ones in the waiting room. I yearn to say something to her that can help. Yet, I do not know how long her daughter has been ill, or if she is receiving any help with the challenges her daughter's condition will present each and every day of her life.

I move a little closer to her and ask, "How long has your daughter been ill?"

She looks at me with surprise, knowing I comprehend and am openly asking this question. She sighs deeply as she decides to respond, "It has been about three years. My husband and I forced her into hospitalization for a week so she could be evaluated. As a result, medications were prescribed. Yet, she is angry at having to take the pills and often refuses them." She looks at her hands now twisting in her lap then adds, "I am hoping she will continue taking the medication and that it can give her a normal life."

I am struck, knowing such hope will no doubt be dashed. Medications available for people with mental illness rarely bring satisfactory change in their lives; at least, not a change that is dependable and definite.

Before speaking, I pray inwardly to know what I can say that might bring meaning to our connection. As I slip my business card to her, I say, "I have worked with people suffering from mental illness within my role as a hospital chaplain. And, I have a friend whose daughter is about the same age as your daughter. She often shares her journey with me. Here is what I can tell you in these brief moments before I am called in to see my dentist. You will probably need help. Do you know about NAMI?"

"No. What is it?"

"NAMI is a national organization with chapters in most cities. The acronym stands for National Alliance on Mental Illness. The purpose of NAMI is to provide support to family members and friends of those struggling with mental illness. I assure you that NAMI's Family-to-Family Program can make a considerable difference to you, your daughter, and all who love her. NAMI also provides support to the 'consumer,' a term used for a person who has mental illness. Their classes offer a wealth of coping skills and other helps to improve life for all involved."

I hear my name as I am now called in to see my dentist. The woman takes a piece of paper from her purse and quickly jots down the acronym NAMI. I recall in that moment the true meaning of sympathy. It is to "fellow-feel" with another person. This happens during the few moments this mother and I encounter one another and touch briefly on one of life's most difficult realities. We are strangers speaking quickly and honestly. Yet, our few words hold promise for changing how this family copes with a very difficult illness.

I see grief in her eyes, but also gratitude as she says, "Good-bye." I carry her in my heart, knowing hers is a grief most parents will not have to bear; nor will they comprehend the path this woman now travels. She will often fear what others think of her daughter, as few will know how to be comfortable with her behavior as they encounter her. This young woman, for the most part, will be socially impoverished. It is likely she will not hold a job for long, and she will rely on her family in many ways. Even so, families often find they cannot adequately meet the needs of a person who is mentally ill.

I feel chagrin as I leave the dentist's office, realizing the road that lies ahead for this family. I recall the words of another woman who also has a daughter with mental illness. Her child, now an adult, was born during the 1960s. Elsie[11] tells of the challenging question asked of her by one of her closest friends: "Say

---

[11] When names or initials are used within this book these have been changed to protect the privacy of individuals. Circumstances are also changed, within this writing, to assure individuals are not identified.

amniocentesis had existed before your daughter's birth. If before the third trimester of your pregnancy you discovered she would suffer so much throughout her life, do you think you would have opted to have an abortion?"

Elsie was not able to answer her friend. She said, "I was so shook up! I could only look at my friend in shock! Her question portrayed her dislike for and judgment of my daughter. She thinks death would be better for her! Our friendship shifted from that day on. I can't help feeling differently about her now, as I believe my friend thinks mental illness warrants being wiped away in the womb. She obviously can't see the love I have for my daughter–and the beauty I see in her young soul. I could *never* wish my child dead."

I could tell she was not finished, so I asked, "I surmise there is something more bothering you as you speak of this, Elsie."

"Yes," she answered, "I wonder how many *other* people think this way about me and the daughter I brought into the world." This is a question she lives with because of one friend's thoughtless question. Elsie told of a similarly painful experience after seeking the help of a counselor hoping for insights and coping skills, as her daughter was experiencing more paranoia and more anger than usual.

Elsie said, "After a third counseling session the counselor looked at me intently, then said, 'Perhaps you will be happy to know that before long, doctors will be able to tell parents the genetic predisposition of their unborn children.' Totally out of touch with my feelings, he continued, 'Then children with mental illness will be aborted.' I did not return for any more of his kind of 'help!'" Then with tears, Elsie added, "I was shook hard by my friend's question. But my counselor's words *really* rocked me back. I couldn't help thinking of Germany and the Nazi crimes."

Chapter Four

*"What is the natural reaction
when told you have a hopeless mental illness?
That diagnosis does you in; that, and the
humiliation of being there. I mean, the
indignity you're subjected to. My God!"*
Kate Millet

What is it like for you when you see a person who is walking alone about town, or in a park, talking out loud? Do questions arise, like: "Is this person dangerous?" "How are the daily needs of this individual being met?" Or, "What can or should be done for him or her?" And, what about those extended questions, like: "What's this condition like for the parents of this person? If they are alive, are they involved?"

Most people have little understanding of the complications involved with mental illness, unless they have a family member or close friend who is mentally ill. For that reason, the story of Sonja, whose daughter lives with mental illness, is told in this chapter. As I ponder elements of her story, Mother Theresa's words come to mind: "People with AIDS are the poorest of poor." There is no doubt that suffering from AIDS or mental illness strips all these people in drastic ways. However, those having mental illness are considerably less fortunate. Their poverty is more extensive. It is nearly impossible for our society to comprehend how to meet their needs. Satisfactory answers seem beyond our reach.

Still, in Matthew 25:31-46, Jesus speaks poignantly, revealing the expectations the Lord has for His followers to make sure the needs of "the least of these among you" are met. While the problem is mammoth for families facing such a horrendous health dilemma, there is something that can be done, and there are certain things that *should not be done*, or said. You saw this in Elsie's words shared earlier within the Pastoral Incident prior to this chapter. You will see it now as Sonja tells her story:

"My youngest child, Elizabeth, came into this world as a happy, chubby baby full of joy. I was 25 at her birth, having married at age 20. The babies came fast. But, by the time of this second conception, it was evident that my marriage was over. I remember thinking adamantly, '*I don't want another baby! I want a divorce!*' Yet, a divorce was not to come for three more years.

"Being happy about the pregnancy was impossible. A month before my due date, a medical emergency required my being hospitalized and placed on medication to stabilize my heart. My cardiologist spoke frankly, 'There is no way for us to know what affect this drug will have on your baby.' It took some moments for me to register those words. So, he rephrased it, 'Sonja, there isn't enough research to indicate what effect this drug may have on a child in the womb.' I was urged to stay on the medication, as he explained, 'You most likely will not survive without it.'

"I had another child to consider. In view of this fact, I opted to be moved immediately from a Catholic hospital into another where my life could come first.

"I prayed, '*Lord, please let my baby live, unless this drug has harmed her and she cannot be whole and healthy. If she is harmed in a way that will make her life very difficult, please take the child to be home in heaven with You.*' When the baby was close to full term, I believed she could do well if I could bring her to birth. My heart told me, *you can trust God. God alone sees the future and knows what is best for this child.*

"I was eight-and-a-half months pregnant when the cardiologist said, 'Based on yesterday's EKG, your pregnancy must be terminated.' Labor was induced the following morning. Fortunately, both Elizabeth and I survived labor and delivery. Upon first sight I named her and loved her.

"As she grew, Elizabeth was delightful, loving, and highly intelligent. At age five, she began using my sewing machine to make clothes for her dolls. I was amazed at how creative she was!

"My divorce became final when Elizabeth was three years old. During the following year, I remarried to a wonderful man. Richard and I enjoyed each of the children, wondering, 'What will this child do in life?' Our lives together brought wonderful times. Early in grade school it was obvious that Elizabeth's intelligence was far above normal. *Surely she has something important to offer the world*, I thought. Then, as Elizabeth approached fourteen, she said, 'Mom, I want to be in the military when I grow up. Military intelligence is so interesting!' At first, Richard and I surmised this was a temporary idea. But Elizabeth showed us articles on military intelligence. She was intrigued through learning how this branch of the military often saves the lives of many soldiers. Already, she had learned the basics of two foreign languages. I thought, *maybe this will be the direction God has for this amazing daughter.*

"Then, as Elizabeth entered her mid-teens, behaviors showed up that did not fit the norm. She was antagonistic and hurt others at times without thinking about what she was doing. Within her teens she began mentally 'leaving' us. Her personality changed gradually. And these changes were major. No longer the happy, humorous girl, now Elizabeth lived isolated within herself most of the time. It was as if she were a different person, one with whom I could not relate. Consequently, it felt like this daughter had left us.

"Not long after that, Elizabeth was diagnosed with schizophrenia: the Grim Reaper, or so it seemed to me. In many ways,

Elizabeth's life was taken from her and from us. She had no choice in the matter, nor did I.

"I read as much as possible hoping to understand schizophrenia. For centuries, the causes of illnesses such as schizophrenia, bipolar disorder, or other forms of mental illness were unknown. In the Bible, people with mental illness were thought to be demon possessed. Later, doctors leaned toward blaming the mother. They claimed the mother had not bonded well with her child. As decades passed, research proved mental illness is a *physical disease* as surely as cancer and heart disease are illnesses of the body. Mental illness comes when a person's brain chemistry goes awry, causing biochemical changes that originate from somewhere within the genetic chain of the person. For our daughter, the illness came on gradually. She was diagnosed by age 18.

"It took several years to fully accept the fact that, yes, Elizabeth is mentally ill. To say that I prayed for Elizabeth's mind to be healed is an understatement. Yet, those many prayers for her to be spared the devastation of mental illness were not answered. Accepting that fact was very difficult while also maintaining faith in a merciful, caring God.

"After years of hoping and praying, my grief and inner angst came to a head. One cold winter day I dialed my friend, Susan. Sorrow had reached an explosive level in my soul. As soon as I heard her voice, I blurt out, 'My daughter is dead!'

"Susan is silent. No doubt she thinks a tragedy has taken place. I can barely breathe while feeling the pain of this recognition. *Yes! It is true.* My friend listens until I can get beyond sobbing out the grief of realizing my teenage daughter is not the person I knew her to be before this illness. For sure, I have to grieve the loss of 'My Elizabeth' before I can love the daughter who is with us.

"'Will you go with me while I bury the dress she made for her Senior Prom?' I ask. Susan knows Elizabeth worked on this beautiful dress off and on for months prior to becoming ill. While making it, she talked happily of the Prom and her dreams of what that night would be like. Now, school is over for Elizabeth. She quit school three months before the end of her 12th year when she could no longer endure the bullying and harassment of certain students. Elizabeth has no plans, now. Her hopes are dashed and her grief over being ill brings bouts of raging, followed by tears. Her sorrow is great. No one dares speak of the Senior Prom. Susan knows the Prom dress represents *my dreams* for my daughter launching out toward success in life. Those dreams are now in slivers like that of a mirror shattered by a blow.

"Susan carefully convinces me not to *literally* bury the Prom dress, saying, 'Wait. She might want to wear it at a family wedding someday.' My dear friend, Susan, is always so practical and powerful with her help. A good listener she is!

"I say, 'Okay, Susan, but will you meet me at the cemetery on Green Brier Hill? I have this place in mind for a ceremony that may help me work through my need to bury my hopes; otherwise, it feels like they will kill me!' A need for closure is grinding my teeth. Susan agrees, although there is snow on the ground and it is bitterly cold. To me, that does not matter. The agony I feel inside cannot be matched.

"When I arrive at the cemetery, there Susan is, waiting. I think, *what a wonderful, faithful friend.* We both get out of our cars. We hug and I point to the monument of The Unknown Soldier.

"That's where we need to go," I say, nodding toward the statue.

"Once there, we use our boots to shovel snow away until we can see the brown, icy dirt. Then, with a small trowel, I weep while digging enough space for five small, smooth stones that I brought from home. I push beyond the tears and the pain, telling myself *it's the only way to move forward.*

"Now I am ready. I begin to bury the stones, one by one. Each represents an element of myself that holds me in bondage: anger, pride, bitterness, envy, and self-pity. One by one these hard stones merge with the icy ground. Burying all five stones allows me to symbolically give them, and Elizabeth, over to God.

"I pray while standing in the shadow of the Unknown Soldier, as this statue represents my daughter more than anything could possibly portray. I pray to release the anger I have over my child's illness. I also pray to understand God, who seems to have turned a deaf ear to my prayers for Elizabeth's life to be different. I want to be healed in my spirit. And, it is time to release my fear: that I have somehow caused Elizabeth's illness through my pregnancy complications that resulted in my taking questionable medications while she was still in my womb. I pray to let go all thoughts that I failed to bond well with her. For, while she was still a tiny infant, I continued to be seriously sick for months beyond her birth. My envy has to go, too, in view of other mothers' whose daughters are Elizabeth's age. It is painful watching as the neighborhood youths are dating and planning toward graduating from high school. Several moms in the neighborhood talk on and on about colleges or jobs that their children are excited about. Standing in the shadow of the Unknown Soldier, I pray to let all this go. I want to be strong, able to help Elizabeth bear the life she now has.

"Before leaving the cemetery, Susan and I hug, while thanking God together for long moments. As I say 'good-bye' to Susan and start my car, I know this is a turning point, one where I can let go the past and begin to accept Elizabeth for the young woman she is. Love is, and always was, there for us; yet, it has taken time and effort to keep letting go of hindrances represented by those five small stones. Gradually, my inner war with her illness became less threatening. Still, although decades have past now, I cannot be comfortable with this thing that 'took her life,' as this is what it looks like to me. Maybe acceptance will come at some point. Meanwhile, love is stronger than the kind of 'death' I feel within my experience of my dear daughter.

"A counselor once said to me, 'Your grief is a *limbo loss*. It is a loss with which you cannot fully reckon, as there is no burial.' Yes. Mental illness is a grief that is impossible to resolve when a person 'leaves' in this way. There is no closure. Since mental illness is a subject that most people don't understand, almost no one is able to walk alongside a parent or family member to offer emotional comfort and support. My friend Susan is an exception.

"Although I buried the 'stone' of pride back at the cemetery, this foe persists. Pride causes me, at times, to be ashamed of my daughter's behaviors. Sometimes, I cringe when others see her talking out loud to herself or laughing at something that is going on in her inner thoughts–her 'other world'–the world beyond ours. Elizabeth has a reality in which none of us are included. We have no place there. As her family, we have to wait for Elizabeth to come back to us when she 'leaves' to be in a world that is foreign to us. As her mother, I fear knowing there are ways in which that world is not a friendly place for her. Times of great fear, called 'paranoia,' come and go for Elizabeth.

"Self-discipline carries me through many challenging moments with Elizabeth, while also bearing the sharp bite of grief. Anger comes within the process of grief, and I have worked through a lot of it. Sometimes, my best intentions for acceptance and understanding lose out. I shout at her, '*Think* before you do things!' Then I feel guilty and ashamed–again. How *hard* her life is. And, it is hard for me to defeat the belief that in some way I failed this child.

"The only way to succeed in this situation is to *walk out* the course of mental illness to its end, as I have found no way to turn its powerful tide. Unresolved grief plows on and is invisible to others. The emotional cost is often a '10' on the 1-10 scale, continually peppering the recesses of my psyche. There are 'cuts, bruises and scars' that only I can feel and see. Many times, I have to say, *OK, God, show me how to handle myself as I watch the devastation in this daughter's life.* My dependence on God being with me day-by-day becomes stronger as I keep my eyes on that reality. God never leaves me, and treats me tenderly, as I'm continually forced to look at my pride, my impatience and my meager level of wobbling acceptance.

"Usually, people feel so inept with mental illness that they find ways to avoid being around it. Or, while with Elizabeth, they pretend it doesn't exist. Only a few people ever ask, 'How is Elizabeth doing?' Except for the professionals who work to try to relieve mental illness, almost no one wants to hear about what's happening in your heart and your home when mental illness exists there. Family members have passed the matter off with, 'Oh, that's just Elizabeth.' They are not able to allow space for validating her struggles, or mine. Inwardly, they may wonder. Yet, they don't ask. Perhaps to do so would make it real to them. So, this suffering must remain hidden for the most part. There is no real hiding it, though, as the disease plays itself out daily, regardless of who is around! If only others had 'eyes' to see what all this means to us.

"Elizabeth is now in her 30s. As the years passed, I did not think to ask Elizabeth if she found life to be meaningful. Nor have I asked her if she finds purpose in her life. I was reticent to do so. Perhaps I feared the question would hurt her, or that her answer would be too hard for me to bear. Recently, I decided to stop making assumptions and ask the question.

"Elizabeth responded openly without hesitation. She said, 'Yes, I am glad to be alive. I do find purpose in my life.' She then shared how her thoughts and ideas are what keep her going. She uses her creative mind, and always hopes one day to invent and patent something useful for others. My soul is enriched by her words. Love and the desire to give are very much alive in Elizabeth. These are God's qualities in her.

"There is sorrow in knowing my daughter's childhood dream of being an intelligence officer are truncated by this dreadful illness. Yet, I see God at work in me *through her* as I am shaped, sharpened, and pulled further and further into spiritual growth and healing. This is true for Elizabeth as well. Although not a single day is easy for her, nothing can match her determination, courage, and hope."

Sonja looks pensive as she nears the end of her story. Then she adds: "At this time, the journey with Elizabeth has involved thirty-one years of watching her struggles, and seeing her through many dilemmas, while helping her bear the burden of her ever-present losses. Through the years, I have felt a huge sense of helplessness that comes and goes. I research the topic as much as my mind can bear. Armed with information, I feel an urgency to make this knowledge available to others. But who wants to know?"

Sonja's life with Elizabeth provides knowledge that is seldom of interest within her circle of friends. She rarely feels able to talk to them about her concerns. While Sonja and her family do everything possible to be certain Elizabeth has a home and the necessities of life, Sonja carries grief over knowing that severe mental illness plagues the majority of people who idly roam our city streets. Sonja wishes more services, than are currently in place, can be provided for those who are so maligned by society. Lots of homeless people are no longer connected with their families. Many of them have two diagnoses: mental illness, combined with an addiction to alcohol or drugs. These substances are crutches used to help them deal with their lot in life. Thankfully, Elizabeth chose not to go that route. She leans on her family, and her church is a great place of strength for her.

Statistics show that mental illness affects *one in five* families like Sonja's. Finding physical comfort in life is difficult for people with this illness, but that is *not* the harshest part of their lives. By far, the worst is that they, at times, live within their minds where mental and emotional agonies follow uncontrollable thoughts. Some hear enticing voices that are sometimes startling and even commanding. It is difficult, at points, for them to keep this inner reality separate from the "real" world you and I are in–the one they must live in. They cannot feel comfortable in their own skins. And, rarely do they feel loved or loveable. Their minds have become their enemies putting many of them through the terrors of paranoia. For some, this goes on every day of their lives and often during the night. The great pleasure of sleeping peacefully is unavailable to many who are mentally ill.

Medications do, at least in part, bring a measure of help *to some*. But currently, medications hold no cure. Almost always, those who do take psychotropic medication find an additional agony of having to go from one drug to another in hopes of gaining dependable help. Most often people quit taking their medication, as they *don't feel themselves* while on them. And, their hopes for help are perpetually dashed. Sonja's daughter Elizabeth is among those who have not found help from psychotropic drugs, at least not much and not for long.

My friend Sonja and I have frequent conversations. The last time we talked, she said, "From what we have endured as a family, it is evident that even well-educated people can be flip about the mentally ill, the poor, or the homeless. People, including those in the media, can be exceedingly cruel for the sake of getting a laugh. They have no comprehension of what it feels like to a person who lives with the effects of mental illness. They think nothing of tromping thoughtlessly over one of the greatest agonies that life can bring."

In my work as a chaplain, I see clearly that one of the worst difficulties people with mental illness experience is that very few can hold a job. This means they will not be able to live well, or even adequately, unless their families are able to help them. They look on as other people live comfortably, experiencing various levels of happiness. Without money, they meet with multiple and continual burdens. They exist mostly isolated and socially impoverished. People either fear them or simply do not want to be around them.

As for fearing them, it is important to know that people with mental illness are many times more likely to be harmed than to victimize others. Statistics show an exceedingly small percentage of people who are mentally ill perpetrate crimes.

As you read this chapter, have you thought of someone you know who has severe mental illness? Or, does your mind go to a parent of such a person? Most of us wonder, "What can be done about this?" It is normal to not want to involve ourselves with a matter so hard to understand—one with which we think we are unable to make a difference. In facing mental illness, there is a sense of helplessness. It is easy to look the other way, as it is difficult to know how to respond. Yet, there is something we can do. We can pray for: 1) researchers who are working to create more effective psychotropic medications, 2) more money to reach them in this research, and 3) families who have children living with this health dilemma.

Some families have two or more children with severe mental illness. These families have little means for dealing with such vast devastation that hits them head-on. We can also pray for greater awareness within society regarding the truth that mental illness is caused by a chemical imbalance in a person's brain, and that it is *a physical condition*. People with mental illness are not defective. They are sick. And, there are ways in which they need our help. For one, we don't need to shun them. We all know what a difference it makes when people extend a smile, or offer words, that show they care about us.

Sonja said, "Our daughter knew early on that marriage and children would not be a good option for her." So, her family-of-origin is her world. With them, she is loved. Yet, Elizabeth's behavior can create trouble between her and her older brother. To say that life is hard for her is an understatement, as mental illness continues to exist on all levels for Elizabeth: Social poverty, financial poverty, emotional poverty, mental poverty, and even physical poverty, as she has an arthritic condition that causes daily pain. Sonja and her husband help Elizabeth as much as they are able, although there are limits as to how much they can do for her.

Finally, Sonja spoke of the sadness she feels in remembering Elizabeth's childhood desire to be an officer in the military. She said, "In time, I came to terms with this, because I now *see* Elizabeth's gift to us all. Every person who encounters her has a choice to make. They can either be kind and helpful, or they can 'dis' her. I am blessed now when I see someone giving Elizabeth a respectful 'hello' with a smile that says, 'You matter. You count.' Or, when someone takes time to talk with her."

Mental illness is a condition that is present in every society. It stands out, persistently forcing us to look at our limits. We can ask for "eyes to see" how we might make life easier for the people who are suffering such grave disadvantages. We can ask for God's perspective and God's leading. Some are called to the mental health field where, within their careers, they can make a difference for these dear, hurting people.

Sonya said something that says a lot about her faith. She said, "As I am forced to witness Elizabeth's daily trials and unending difficulties, I 'see' with eyes that want not to see. What is true, too, is that although this illness is something I would never choose to happen to my child, goodness comes to my life through Elizabeth. Elizabeth has a purpose on this earth. And, after this life, our family will reunite in the presence of God. There, Elizabeth's ministry to us will be seen clearly. We each will know Elizabeth for who she is to us now, and who she truly will be for us in eternity. There, I believe, we will stand in awe when we truly get the picture."

This mother's faith in God's love and God's noble purposes holds everything together for her. And, granted, her faith is often tested! Elizabeth, too, lives out her faith. She trusts God to help her day-by-day. On rare occasions, her parents see Elizabeth having conversation with individuals who show openness to her. Usually, these are strangers. When this happens, Sonja and Richard see joy and hope in her face. These are moments when each of their hearts is touched.

Pastoral Incident # 5

Joe [12] is dissatisfied with himself. He feels buried in life's circumstances. He is angry and hurt. Men don't talk in counseling sessions as easily as women. But, Joe's doctor is urging him to talk with me. At first he seems unable to reveal what brings him to my office. Given time, Joe finds the words to reveal his stress and the burden of high powered emotions.

He struggles to get the words out, then says, "My wife...I love the woman, but I'm afraid she will leave me. At times, she seems understanding. At other times, she is distant; she gets angry because of our financial struggles. Seems we are about to drown in debt. I know she is under stress. I get hurt and angry, though, when she spews, claiming I am a failure, unable to support my family.

Early in life, Joe followed his father into construction work. They are good at what they do. But, now in his early 50s, Joe is recovering from a heart attack followed by open heart surgery. This temporarily ends the only work he knows how to do. Meanwhile, the bills are piling up. He said, "I really need to do a different kind of work. The truth is *I want* different work!"

Joe tells of knowing there is no way he can go to school, at this point. There are four children in the family, his truck is about to be repossessed, and his wife's income does not cover their monthly expenses. I am seeing Joe within private practice–not in a hospital setting– we can work together with the coming weeks. I finally get him to talk about his feelings.

He says, "I have a lot of fear. And, I am sad that I can't do better by my family. I get angry at my circumstance and I'm disappointed that life can't be different than it is!"

We spend some time with techniques for handling difficult

---

[12] When names or initials are used within this book these have been changed to protect the privacy of individuals. Circumstances are also changed, within this writing, to assure individuals are not identified.

emotions, while also exploring his spiritual life and what it means to Joe.

"I am a Christian. I go to church, pay tithes, and I desire God's will."

"Why do you believe we are here, Joe?" I can see he knows I am referring to why we are here *on earth.*

Some clients have a difficult time coming up with an answer to this question, but Joe speaks quickly, "We are to serve. I mean, we are to help others." He thinks for a minute, and then adds, "I know that is true. But what am I doing in construction work? We build high-rises for wealthy land owners. I can't see how my part in this work fulfills my purpose on earth!"

"Joe, would you tell me about your goals?"

"I need to get back to work." He looks down. I wait. "But the truth is I am terribly tense about having to continue in construction work."

"As you see it, Joe, what are your options?"

"The only option I see is to get well, return to work, and then dig my way through the debt we are now accumulating."

I probe for more and seem to get nowhere. What eventually comes out is that there is a desire that is woven solidly within Joe's soul. He says, "I want to do something different with my life. I no longer want to work for a paycheck. I want to use my time in ways that help people who are in need."

"Tell me more about how you see that happening." I ask.

He can't see any options. Joe has no training for a profession that would allow him to earn his living within social services. Based on what skills he has Joe sees himself as stuck with construction work. I wonder how we can get beyond this. I often have to curb the urge to make a suggestion. But, this is Joe's work. He does not need a rescuer.

"I can hardly stomach returning to a job that I no longer have a desire to do. My heart simply aches to be involved with work that is meaningful...doing something that makes a difference in the lives of people who are really in need."

"When you think about doing something to help others, what comes to your mind?" I ask.

"Well, I can't earn my living at it, but Christmas is around the corner. I'm good with mechanics...I'm thinking of kids who need bicycles—maybe there are some adults without cars that could use a good bicycle." Joe takes his time while forming an idea of how he could volunteer to repair, or rebuild, bicycles during the six-weeks of recovery his doctor is asking of him.

"What do you feel when you talk about this possibility, Joe?"

"It brings hope. I like this idea." His voice sounds stronger as he speaks.

"I recall something said within a workshop a few years back," says Joe. "The speaker said, 'It doesn't take a lot of what we want or need; it only takes a little bit to satisfy a longing.' She was talking to us about balancing our work, with play, encouraging participants to add frequent activities into our lives that bring us pleasure."

He adds, "That makes me think about the fact I could tolerate construction work more easily if I take some evenings, here and there, to continue that volunteer work."

"Ah. Are you saying the way you feel about construction work could be affected by that?" I ask.

"Yes." Joe's face looks so much lighter. "It won't pay my bills, but it is true that money isn't everything. I'm going to carry through with this idea we are talking about, Chaplain Joy, but I *really, really want* to be more involved with God's work. I just read the 25th Chapter of Matthew the other day. Wow! Does the Lord ever make clear the importance of serving people who are in need! And, people who are in trouble."

Then it happened. I hear words coming out of my mouth and without thinking about a single one of them I say, "Joe, when you want with all your heart to do something good in life, yet your circumstance does not allow it, in God's eyes it is as if you have done it." We look at one another for a long moment. This is an aha moment. Each of us realizes those words are God's truth to him.

Many times within my work, I've experienced the Holy Spirit doing a "takeover" like that. During those moments, I've heard words spill from my mouth carrying a message that surprisingly teaches me as well as the person I am ministering to. Every time, there is a certain thrill, as I know God is real and God is *for us*! God is *with* us!

Chapter Five

*"He who dwells in the secret place
of the Most High shall abide
under the shadow of the Almighty."*
Psalm 91:1

Joe moved forward with his plan to do charitable work while he healed. He also decided to read the Bible in its entirety for the first time. We continued doing inner healing work. Within a few weeks, he was back on the job working on another high rise. The enjoyment Joe found in reconstructing bicycles grew through meeting some of the people who received them. This encouraged him to find a little time each week for this volunteer work. Meanwhile, Joe showed excitement over all he was learning while diligently reading Scripture.

One day, Joe calls. "Chaplain Joy, listen to this!" He is excited–but in a not-so-happy way. "I just now read something that disturbs me in Matthew 5:48, 'Be perfect, therefore, as your heavenly Father is perfect.' What in the world does *this* mean? I can't be perfect!"

He is waiting on the line. So, I take a big breath with a quick inner prayer before speaking. "Lord, help me to know what Joe needs to hear on this."

I respond, "Joe, it means to turn your life over to God and let Him do the rest."

Joe isn't satisfied with that, for which I am glad. He then says, "But it can't *be that simple.* I've always feared not measuring up in life—and this proves I can't make it!"

"I see that directive in the Bible, too, Joe. Hold the phone a minute. I want to locate where I recently read that in an Old Testament passage. Here it is, in Leviticus 22:32, 'Do not bring shame to my name, for I will display my holiness...I am the Lord who makes you holy.' Here, God is saying *He makes us holy.* We can't do it in our own efforts."

As Joe listens, I trust the words as they come to me. "Listen to the words of Jesus as He prays to the Father for all His disciples in the 17th Chapter of John, 'I in them, and You in Me; that they may be made perfect in one, and that the world may know that You have sent Me, and have loved them as You have loved Me.' Jesus was praying for us to be made perfect *in God*, as we *become One* with God. This is a *process* through which *we become* holy. And, God is in charge of it. He does the work in us. Perfection is what we reach as *we cooperate* with God's work in us. This is how we move within the process of *becoming* holy. It takes patience to believe it is happening."

Joe says, "I think I'm getting it. The word 'holy' throws me, though. I can't comprehend thinking of myself as holy."

"Holiness is what we are growing into, Joe. In the Scriptures it is clear what shameful behavior is. The more we read Scripture, the more we see what pleases God and what displeases God. Our consciences become more informed in this way. The Holy Spirit sharpens our consciences, telling us when we are not living in ways that bless our families and others. It is through repentance and correcting our behavior that we are restored into holy living. It truly is an amazing journey—and it is an awesome adventure. For sure, the greatest adventure of all! We were created for this."

Joe is quiet and I feel we are not quite finished. "While this work goes on, Joe, God sees us as we *shall be* once our lives and our growth are complete. This is a wondrous gift of God's grace to us! Holiness is linked with being in an intimate relationship with God in which we are continually making choices. This doesn't mean we will always make good choices or that good choices are made through our own efforts. If we pursue holiness on our own, this will result in pride, and create an attitude of self-righteousness. We will be inclined to judge others, seeing ourselves as better than they are. But, if we choose to grow in intimacy with God, holiness results."

When I hang up, I am amazed. It took only a few minutes for Joe to grasp the essence of holiness. I, too, am blessed through revisiting a subject that has always been challenging to me, as well.

Joe calls for an appointment two weeks later. He wants to talk about the shame he feels over some things he has done that haunt him. I am quiet while he talks, then I say, "Joe, as Christians, remember it is Christ who is our Savior. We can't save ourselves from the wretched things we do. When you read Isaiah, you will find these powerful words, 'Come now, and let us reason together, says the Lord, Though your sins are like scarlet, they shall be as white as snow; though they are red like crimson, they shall be as wool.' You can find that passage in Isaiah 1:18. As you can see, I have memorized that one. It holds power for me in my life as I too have remorse over things done—and not done—in the past."

This is a short session. I ask him to take the rest of the hour to ponder the passage in Isaiah, saying, "Joe, rejoice in the Lord over the truth that you *can let the past go*. And, notice the flow of new and pleasant energy that comes to your body as you persist in this act of rejoicing! God created us to enjoy entering into His presence with praise and thanksgiving."

"That sounds great!" he says. "I think I'll take a walk by the river. This way, while I celebrate, I can sit and listen to the fish jump."

Joe's struggles are common for all of us. We do make poor choices and outright mistakes—even some that are alarming, and so we cry, Oh, *God! I can't believe I did that*! When we see what we have done, and confess it, we are back in the state of "righteous," which in simple language means "right-doing." Our journey in holiness continues. It is not our holiness. It is God's holiness that we walk in. We see this while reading about the lives of God's people throughout the Bible. Remorse and, at times, even chastisement are part of the journey. I have experienced God's woodshed. You probably have been there at points, too. Right? It is a place where we feel terrible while our conscience works us over. But, we don't have to stay there! Mistakes can be our best teachers once we repent and move on!

It is *our love for the Lord* that makes us inclined to say "no" to what our hearts tells us is displeasing to the Lord. And, it is our love for the Lord that sees us wanting to do what is right and good. Central to this walk is preferring God's will over our own. Here, we are living in the spiritual kingdom that Jesus called "the kingdom of God." This adventure is *exceedingly wonderful*. Still, it is not easy—and challenges us quite often. It is an adventure of transformation based on mutual love. The Lord draws us like a magnet into wanting to enter, and live into, that "secret place" Scripture speaks of, wherein we are to abide. And, our spirits are lifted up as we realize there is no need to strive for our Lord's acceptance. We have it *already*!

Through ever-pressing forward, we enter into what Brother Lawrence, a saint of the past, wrote in *Practice of the Presence of God*.[13] This was a man who lived in a priory, washing dishes and repairing sandals during the 17th Century. Yet, his profound peace and joy attracted many visitors who sought his spiritual guidance. Conversations with Brother Lawrence, and segments of his letters, became the basis for the book titled *The Practice of the Presence of God*. This is a powerful little book for people who want to live more and more fully into what is possible for us.

One day, Joe came to a counseling session feeling low and somewhat anxious. I suggest that he journal on his thoughts and feelings, which often brings us into a better place emotionally—especially if we also write about the things we are

---

[13] Brother Lawrence (a Carmelite monk named Nicolas Herman at birth)," *Practice of the Presence of God* (UK: Spire Books, 1967)

grateful for. I said, "Joe, I have been pondering the words Jesus said to the man who was under the throes of a legion of demons. Would you like to hear that story and how it relates to me?"

He is interested. So, I tell him of how Jesus released this man by cleansing him from the demons. No longer naked, chained, and screaming—and now in his right mind—the man's natural response was to beg to stay with Jesus. Jesus said, "No" to that. He said instead, "Go...tell how much the Lord has done for you, and how He has had mercy on you."

I tell Joe about the time when I wanted to die and did my best to make that happen through attempting suicide, and how God intervened through circumstances beyond my control. "Joe, I heard the Savior's words: 'Stay here; you can't come, yet.' These were the very words He spoke to the man who lived in chains due to his demons. Both of us chose to obey as we heard the Lord's mandate to tell of being healed and to tell others how exceedingly good and merciful is our God. The same Lord who healed the man tormented by demons also healed me, Joe. Only my healing didn't come in an instant; it took time and some real effort on my part. Then, I was ready to *"Go tell."*

Before the session ends, I give him some time to do a journaling assignment. When he leaves, I could tell his spirit is in a far better place.

All of us have our "demons." We can feel the chains that hold us back from being all we can be. I've not murdered anyone or stolen another's property. Yet, beyond that, I've encountered most all other sins. I know I am capable of every one of them. I've chaffed against the chains. *Yet, I am redeemed! Guilt-free.* Knowing this, I love the Lord with all that is in me, and I am *determining* to follow the directives of Jesus, the One who set me free. When I wanted to take my life, Jesus wanted me to stay here to raise my children, be healed, and to find how much I am loved, then to pass that love on to others. The *good news* from God is that the Lord wants to release us from our chains. Are you thinking, *my chains are like tinsel, not much of a bother; I'm happy where I am at*? If so, wait to see if that is where you want to be at the end of this chapter.

During the first few decades of my life, prayer happened for me "on the fly," meaning, in the midst of my achieving "the stuff of life." No doubt God blessed that, but He had something more in mind. I was about to experience an exciting venture with God, one in which prayer became a response to God's movement within my soul. Here is how it all started:

Every morning after getting out of bed I head for the kitchen—and coffee. This trek means passing through a hallway, dining room, then into the kitchen. I pass by the opening to our entry and the off-the-traffic-pattern formal living room. This room is seldom used. What I can see of the living room, as I pass down the hall, is limited. One morning, as I sleepily make my way toward the kitchen, I hesitate slightly. For days, I have noticed something different about that living room. There is an uncanny sense of someone being in that room. So, on this particular morning, I slowly venture into the living room and look around, wondering. Although I cannot see anyone, it definitely feels like someone is here. I ask out loud, "Is this You? Lord, *are You in here?*"

Instantly, I feel resounding "warmth" in my heart. Then, in the midst of this sense of "Presence," I hear these words spoken, "Come, and be with me." I know these words are not from my thought. I sit down, nonplussed, yet deeply touched. I begin to let my heart sink into the presence of the Lord. I feel superbly appreciative in perceiving that God indeed desires my company. How can I doubt it, given this kind of invitation!

From then on, for several years, I went into that room first thing every morning seeking to encounter God's presence. It was a wonderful time for experiencing prayer, finding it to be less about talking and more about listening. Reading the Scriptures held a prominent place during this time with the Lord. I listened to what God wanted me to hear—and to live out. Sometimes, I would weep, as the presence of the Lord was felt so strongly.

Once in the middle of the night, I felt an encouraging nudge to get out of bed and to be with the Lord instead of sleeping. Then, I notice the living room light comes on. I know this was strange. Maybe I imagined that light flipping on.

So, I wake up Gary, saying, "Did you leave the living room light on?"

He said, "No. Go back to sleep."

Still, I know that light was not on when we went to bed. So, I get up and go into the living room. I sit. There is that usual sense of being joined by the Lord. Then, I hear these words, "I want to teach you." I am amazed, so stay on. By then, I lose all interest in sleeping. I become very still, simply worshiping in the silence of the night. Then, words begin to come into my mind like little rivulets of water, flowing gently and surely. I quickly take up paper and pen so these words can be captured. As soon as I finish writing a sentence or two, more words are there, waiting to be written. I write throughout the rest of the night.

Looking back, I think of that night as a training session. I filled a book, just from listening, as simple, short sentences entered my mind. Most were pieces of wisdom. In the morning I showed these to Gary. Some seemed profound. While using a typewriter, he created unique and interesting art to accompany these sayings. Here is an example of one such saying with Gary's original artwork

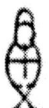  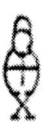

Just as you enjoy the various birds on the wing, take pleasure in the different species of people on the world's scene.

This began a serious and life-changing quest for me. I became more and more involved in prayerful listening. While worshiping during these times, I realized endorphin flows [14] come while rejoicing in the Lord! For a number of years, I spent the first two hours of every day with the

---

[14] Endorphin flows are caused by chemical changes in the body within very pleasant experiences.

Lord in that room. It was my "place apart," where I could worship, write, and pray. This was not only a wonderful experience, but a lot of inner healing was taking place during this practice. And, this was *reflecting in my physical body*. I was getting well! It was happening ever-so-slowly, through my being obedient to how the Holy Spirit was leading my soul. I called it "My Get Well Program."

In looking back, I know God was preparing me for ministry in chaplaincy. Health and strength were springing up through this daily practice of prayer and listening. I was learning how to hear the voice of the Lord speaking within, which became an essential part of my work in emergency rooms and in trauma settings. There, people are greatly disturbed, in pain, uncertain, and needing God's help. I found I could rely on hearing the Lord guiding and providing what is needed within each situation.

Now, I work mostly in private practice rather than in institutions. I was with a client last month who is drawn to Christianity, but has not yet made a decision to embrace the teachings of Jesus Christ. She said, "I was talking with a friend recently. She said she is 'in the world, but not of it.' That is strange. What does it mean?"

I explained to her that in the Bible there are several places where God makes it clear that we are to be "a peculiar people." This might sound strange, but it refers to our being a people who are chosen. God calls, and when we decide to respond to the message of Christ, we become His disciples. We still live in this world, yet we will handle life differently.

This is addressed in 1 John 2:16, "For all that is in the world—the lust of the flesh, the lust of the eyes, and the pride of life is not of the Father, but is of the world." A Christian devotes her or his life to seeing this world as a temporary place. We know that, after death, God will resurrect us into eternal life with the Lord and all God's people. Meanwhile, we live here on planet earth differently than we did before. We are following what Jesus taught about life and living.

The spirituality we are transported into is what Jesus referred to as "the kingdom of God," defined as "righteousness, peace, and joy in the Holy Spirit." We have times of knowing the lust of the flesh, the lust of the eyes, and the pride of life is a part of all humanity. We deal with these impulses as they come up. Ideally, we choose to resist the temptations to make self-centered choices.

When we choose to follow Christ, we place our trust in Him, and choose a different way of being. Through prayer and confession, righteous living prevails. Then, at our resurrection into eternal life, we will arise like the great Phoenix from the ashes, leaving behind these tendencies that come with being human. The Holy Spirit of God now lives within us to guide and to teach us as we make our way while in this world. Therefore, we are in the world, yet choosing *a different* way of being in the world.

Sometimes I have the thrilling experience of leading a person to Christ within this work. When people are ready, the Holy Spirit is there to lead our conversation. Moving forward too quickly is not a good practice. God has many workers on the field and does not often use me as a "harvester." Most often, I plant seeds, then water them. When seed is planted, it takes time before the hunger and thirst for righteousness grows to the place the person hears that inner call to take up his or her cross and follow Christ.

At times, people resist entering a life of faith, claiming there are too many "conflicts with science." This is well refuted in an article by Francis S. Collins, M.D., Ph.D., the former director of the National Human Genome Research Institute. Dr. Collins is now the director of the National Institutes of Health, and the author of *The Language of God*.[15] As one of the lead scientist in the human genome research project, he writes, "Out of this, we learned an incredible amount of things that were surprises!" In an Internet article Dr. Collins writes, "Science explores the natural world. Faith explores the supernatural world. If I want to study genetics, I am going to use science. If I want to understand God's love, then that is where the faith world comes in ... from my perspective, these two

---

[15] Francis S. Collins, *The Language of God* (New York: Freepress, 2006).

world views coexist."[16]   As a scientist, Dr. Collins says, "I believe that we are enriched and blessed. We have an opportunity to practice science as a form of worship. We have a chance to see God as the greatest scientist."

We are awesomely created.   Consider these thought-provoking photographs provided through the work of C.J. Bassham[17] and Dr. Robert Langridge whose photograph[18] on the right was taken from a "down the barrel" view of the human DNA Double Helix.

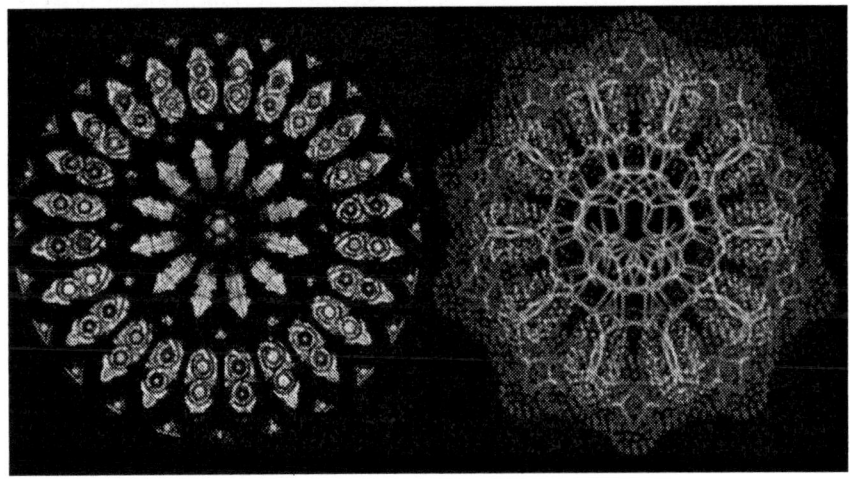

I think of the beautiful imagery, on the right, as the signature of the

---

[16] http://www.asa3.org/ASA/PSCF/2003/PSCF9-03Collins.pdf, visited 2/24/2013.
[17] Photo by C.J. Bassham, photographer, presented within Dr. Francis Collins' Internet article.
[18] Courtesy of Dr. Robert Landridge, Copyright, Regents of the University of California.

Creator, a pattern displayed within all human DNA. These photos show similarity, as the image on the left bears an amazing resemblance to the rose window set in York Minster, a beautiful and imposing gothic cathedral in York, England. Long before science discovered DNA, numerous Christians, throughout the world, built this image in the stained glass windows of their cathedrals. These same geometrical designs closely resemble the ancient mandala used to quiet the mind and open the heart for those desiring the qualities of love, compassion, forgiveness, and peace.

There are multiple signs of God's presence with us here on earth and this image within our DNA indicates something of the beauty God created and is forever creating. As we love and serve Him, we are continuous expressions of the beauty He loves.

The truth is that we were created to worship God and to commune with Him. This was verified in science a few years ago. Three medical researchers found the link between the mind and the spirit of human beings. In their book titled *Brain Science and the Biology of Belief – Why Won't God Go Away,*[19] one of the authors wrote of what was found that amazed them. While using sophisticated imaging devices, Dr. Andrew Newberg, Dr. Eugene D'Aquill, and Vince Rause viewed the brain of individuals in prayer and meditation. As a result, they became convinced that our brains are wired in such a way as to propel human beings forward towards a journey of transformation. The excitement of these authors, as they realize the human brain is wired with "transcendent powers," is notable.

We are to glory in the fact His presence is in us and, therefore, in our journey. We carry it within our very being. Second Corinthians 4:7 shows a truth to hold dear: "We have this treasure in earthen vessels, that the excellence of the power may be of God and not of us." The message from the Lord, here, is clear: You are an expression of my presence on earth.

---

[19] Andrew Newberg, Eugene D'Aquill, and Vince Rause, *Brain Science and the Biology of Belief—Why Won't God Go Away* (New York: Ballantine, 2002).

I reiterate that it is God's longing that we have an *intimate* relationship with Him. This is the place where believers in Christ are invited to live, move, and have their being. It is "the secret place of the Most High"...our spiritual "promised land" while on terra firma. Reaching for this means we are moving into the "kingdom of God," defined in Scripture as "righteousness, peace, and joy in the Holy Spirit." If that sounds too lofty, stop to contemplate Jesus' prayer in John, Chapter 17. In that one chapter, we see something that truly reveals what is intended for us.

We can reach a wondrous place of union with God at points in our journey–then lose hold of it. We reach it, again–*only to lose it, again*! If anything has perpetual motion, this is it! This continues while we gradually mature in our walk with God, growing in our oneness with Him. All the time, God is *the instigator* of this movement in our souls. His affection and desire for us draws us onward. We enter the "secret place" through humility and longing after the Lord. We hear His call, within, to "Come away." We find happiness in setting aside time to be with the Lord. Here is our shelter from the problems of the world. Prayer is a wondrous place of solace that we can enter at any time and in any place. It is a form of love. And, love is the most powerful entity in the world. For, God is love. First John 4:16 makes this ever so clear: "God is love, and he who abides in love abides in God and God in him." Abiding in prayer day-by-day is a life lived in love. Through *this* we bear fruit.

Beyond healing us and forgiving us, the Lord wants to have an integral part of our lives. God is waiting and longing for us to grow in our ability to hear His voice and to trust what we hear. Following God's lead in life, brings great joy–even excitement–as we surmount every obstacle...and savor each mountain top. This is called practicing the presence of God.

I hear people say, "I prayed and nothing happened." Not so. Wait. God knows. God hears! Timing is often a major element. Trust... as God is working out what is best for us–and for others–as to how and when a prayer is answered. There are times when He loves us too much to answer in the precise terms, or timing, in which we ask. Something always happens when we pray, as a spiritual force is set in motion. It is possible to develop a radical willingness to trust God.

God is patient and accepting as we progress up the mountain of life, while enjoying and savoring much that is glorious. And, when the valleys come, we have the strength to press on, knowing righteousness, peace, and joy in the Holy Spirit is our *promised land*. Jesus called it the kingdom of God. Paul's challenge for those of us who want to live in that kingdom of God is to cast down "every high thing that exalts itself against the knowledge of God, bringing every thought into captivity to the obedience of Christ" (2 Cor 10:5). This is an awesome goal. And, it is possible.

Setting our course to reach this state of heart and mind means there will be sacrifice, but oh the wonderment that comes in what is truly the greatest adventure in all of life: finding and living within "the secret place of the Most High under the shadow of the Almighty" (Ps 91:1).

Chapter Six

"Whether you turn to the right or to the left, your ears will hear a voice behind you, saying, 'This is the way; walk in it'"
Isaiah 30:21

The story of our friend, Ed Conforti, illustrates how the message of Chapter Five is lived out by a perfect stranger, after God places a request in his mind. The message of the stranger became what Ed calls "my wake-up call!" Here is Ed's amazing story:

I am going about my business as president of a bank when a stranger walks through the doors and delivers an astounding message—a message that changed my life.

At the time, I was fulfilling my newly acquired position as a bank president in Washington State. Just prior to the stranger's arrival, I was fielding some heavy-duty challenges in my upstairs office.

Actually, things usually went well for me in business. Having good communication and management skills, I could meet my goals and enjoy success most of the time. In fact, I was about as self-reliant as a person can be.

But this year was different. Things had begun to change. The economic environment in the country reflected what was happening in the financial markets. I was feeling the burden of keeping the bank going and seeing that it remained profitable despite a myriad of conditions which, at the time, were threatening to the bank. The pressure had been intense for months. Moreover, I was dealing with the pain of ending a marriage of 29 years. Between the pressure of work and the unresolved issues of my marriage, the fabric of my soul was wearing thin.

Seven months before this, I had visited a Trappist monastery in Utah to clear my head, find some much needed rest. I wanted to solicit the advice of one of the monks who is a close friend and confidant. I shared my feelings with him, including the emptiness I felt due to my divorce and the need for a sense of direction and purpose for my life. In response, he referred me to the biblical account of Paul's conversion on the road to Damascus, found in the ninth chapter of the Book of Acts.

He pointed out the critical part that Ananias played by leading Paul on a course of finding and following God's will. He then suggested that I read this passage in Acts each day, prayerfully asking for an "Ananias" to lead me on a path of God's choosing. My friend promised to remember me at the monastery every day at the 4 a.m. Mass, until our prayers were answered. I committed to be faithful to this request.

June 26, 1979, was the memorable day when things began to happen. The first event of that day took place as a result of the bank's senior loan officer coming into my office.

He said, "Ed, I am thinking about a career change. I want to leave banking. We need to talk."

I did not want to hear this. The man was one of my best people. Things were tough enough. It would hurt me and the bank, if he were to leave.

He broke into my thoughts, saying, "I need some good advice from you, Ed. I need to talk with you as a friend, rather than as the president of this bank."

So I scheduled two hours between 8 and 10 a.m. to meet the next morning. We were to talk about where he was and what his options might be.

Then, as if that were not enough, about 4:30 p.m. the chief financial officer came into my office and closed the door. "Ed," he said, "I'm having severe personal problems. I'm having trouble...I cannot handle my work." With that, he started crying uncontrollably. I did not know what to do, so I stayed with him for the next hour-and-a-half until he could regain his composure.

He asked if we could meet again, saying that he needed to talk out his problems. I assured him that I would meet him at noon the next day at my house and that whatever time he needed I would make that available to him.

As I closed the door of my office that night, there was much on my mind. I had a serious overload. One of my senior people was talking about leaving the bank, and another was having a nervous breakdown.

The next morning, while I am shaving, all the strength suddenly leaves my legs. I fall to the floor. I check myself out mentally. I am not faint or dizzy, so what's the problem, here? There isn't any numbness in my legs. But there is no strength in them.

I begin crawling out of the bathroom into the bedroom, thoroughly puzzled. I try to get onto the bed. The struggle takes 20 minutes. My legs are dead weight. When I finally do succeed in pulling myself up onto the bed, I sit there for long moments trying to figure out what is going on.

Looking at the clock, I remember my appointment with the senior loan officer at 8 a.m. Using every available resource, I push and pull myself forward until I can manage to stand on my feet. Awkwardly, I finish shaving, get dressed, and even drive myself to the office. Feeling shaky, I congratulate myself for at least being back on my feet.

I arrive at the bank at 7:45 a.m. and think I might as well start this meeting early. I had seen the senior loan officer enter the building a few minutes before, so I start down the hall to get him.

Suddenly, my legs go out from under me again, and I slump to the floor.

I am relieved that no one is around to see what just happened. As best I can, I crawl back into my office, push the door shut, and sit on the floor, completely perplexed. For the first time today, I begin to think about the seriousness of the situation.

It occurs to me that I should start to pray. "God, will You please come and help me? Will You clear my head?"

Right then, it comes to me that I had been running my life as if I could solve all my problems by myself. I see in an instant how this is my lifelong pattern. Whenever I ran into difficulties, I had always beaten the problem by working harder, or working longer, or just toughing it out. The habit was formed without regard for the fact that God was the One in charge. With these thoughts, my prayer changes.

"God, I acknowledge that I have been running my life as though I am in charge of everything instead of You. I promise You that I won't do that anymore. From this day forward, I will try to remember that You are the Boss. I am going to tie into You and see You as the source of my strength."

After having said that, I told God that there are three things that I really need this day. "First, I really need my legs. I have a stewardship here at the bank. The employees, the stockholders, the board, and the customers are all depending on me."

I get bold and say, "I need to be able to do my work here. God, I want that strength back right now, and I believe You will answer my prayer. And, while I'm talking to You, I need, above all, to know if You love me. I'm not sure whether You do or not."

I believe that doubt had to do with the guilt that I felt over the failure of my marriage. Am I outside of His love, now? I need to know.

Finally, I tell Him that the morning's happenings brought me to wondering whether or not it is His will for me to be in this bank, doing what I am doing. "I'm here quite by my own choice," I tell God. "And, I am not too sure if this is what You want me to do. So, will You please make it clear to me, somehow, what it is You want me to do? Then, I'll do it."

I thank God for hearing my prayer. As I stand up, I find my legs are good again. It is now 8:00 a.m. Immediately, I go down the hall to get the loan officer for our appointment. We return to my office where we spend the next two hours. Once finished, I start out to meet the operations officer to go over the plans for the construction of a new branch bank.

Just as I move across the reception area, I see a stranger standing by the receptionist's desk. The receptionist is away from her desk, so I stop to ask, "Have you been helped?"

"No, I haven't," the man said,

"I'm sorry," I say, "The secretary is probably in the back room making copies or getting herself a cup of coffee. Tell me who you want to see and I'll direct you there."

"Well, who are you?" the stranger asked.

"I'm Ed Conforti."

"Mr. Conforti, you're the man that I came to see. And I need to see you right now, if you have the time. My name is Jim Dawson."

I said, "Well, okay, I'll see you now, if it's important."

"It is," he said.

I take him to my office, at which time he tells me he is a local real estate broker, and then adds, "I do not know you at all. I just know who you are. I don't even do business with this bank. So, we are complete strangers." He is obviously uneasy.

I close the door to my office. He continues, "Ed, do you believe in God?"

At this point, I begin to wonder about this man, but I answer,

"Well, yes I do."

"That will sure make this a lot easier, because what I have to tell you—well...if you weren't a believer in God, you would probably throw me out."

He seems a bit more comfortable. He begins to tell me about selling a large piece of real estate six months ago and how earlier this morning he had a legal hearing to attend concerning the property. The hearing was scheduled for 9:30 a.m.

"The buyer and seller are suing one another," Jim says, "and I am the broker in the middle of it. I went to my office about 7 o'clock this morning to prepare some notes. Consequently, I was absorbed in thoughts about my testimony. Then suddenly at about 7:45, your name came into my mind. I couldn't understand that, because I did not know you personally. There was no connection. So I tried to push your name out of my mind and get back to my notes."

I think about interrupting him. A different time can be set for us to talk; but I cannot bring myself to do that. He continues, "But you kept coming back into my mind, again and again! So, after the third or fourth time, I just pushed myself back from the desk and gave up on finishing my notes. It seemed fairly likely that God was trying to speak to me about you."

Jim explains that he is a member of one of the churches in town and that he believes that God uses "messengers" to touch the lives of others from time to time. He continues, "I began to talk to God about this. I asked, 'God, is there some reason why this man's name keeps coming into my mind?'"

Jim leans forward and clears his throat. "Now, Ed, I've got some things to tell you. I know, now, that it was the Lord who spoke your name to me this morning. He was urging me to get over here immediately to see you. I knew that, for this one morning, I was to be his personal representative to you. That meant that when I spoke to you, I would be speaking directly from Him."

That was a little heavy, but I let him go on. "Now, this is really going to sound strange, but I've got to say it."

He looks me straight in the eye and breathes deeply. "First of all, I have been told to tell you that you have been making a big mistake all of your life by trying to see yourself as the source of all your strength. You've got to remember that strength comes from the Father, through Jesus and the Holy Spirit. And, I've been told to tell you to keep that in your mind and to operate your life that way from this point on. If you do that, strength will be there when you ask for it."

He asks me if I have that straight, and I say, "Yeah."

"Now, the second thing I have been asked to tell you is how much Jesus loves you."

Right then I am pretty over-awed, but he is not through. Jim says, "He has loved you so much from the moment of your conception—and He has asked me to assure you that you have never been outside His love. He asked me to tell you that."

And lastly, Jim says "I don't know what this one means, but He has asked me to tell you to keep on doing what you're doing now and that He will tell you later what He wants you to do." Then he says, "Ed, does any of this make sense to you?"

I tell Jim the story of what had taken place with me during that same time frame of 7:45 and 8:00 a.m. When I finish, we both fall silent—fully aware that something extraordinary has happened. It is obvious that God had heard my prayers, and those of my monk friend, and is "getting back to me" through Jim.

It feels as if I have found the unlisted number for God, even the area code! I am unspeakably grateful to Jim for his courage and obedience to God's request. And, I am full of joy, sensing how much God loves me.

Jim laughs, "You can't imagine how hard it was to come over to this stuffy old bank and look you up—the president—who didn't even know me, and deliver such a message."

He describes to me how that, after attending the hearing, he had driven to the bank. "I arrived here at about 9:30 a.m. But, I had to park my car in front of the bank three times. Each time I would start the car again and drive away. But then, I would turn around and come back, because it felt as if a force was pushing me towards the bank. Believe me; it took a while to get up enough nerve to carry this out!"

We part with a hug and hardy slaps to the back.

That night I think back to my early twenties, recalling how I read numerous books in hopes of answering my questions: Does God exist, or not? At that time in my life, I came to the place where I felt I had found faith. Still, I questioned, at points, through the years. Now, after my experience with Jim Dawson, I know I will never, ever, have to question again. This is a fact for me, now. From that time on, God was real. He sneaked up on me! Using the face and heart of a man named Jim Dawson, God reached me, leaving no doubt that He loves me and that He wants to guide my life.

From that point on, I am God's man, seeking His direction daily, desiring for God's will to be done in my life rather than my own. Although this "intervention" with Jim Dawson is an unusual one, I have come to a new understanding of the interconnectedness of God's people. For this reason, I listen more and more for the inner directives that are there for me.

Consequently, I too have been used by God through a few words spoken to an employee, a friend, or a family member as "directed by Love." Such moments have sparked life and truth, consolation and hope, at times, when I knew God was again at work.

Each day has become an adventure as I watch for opportunities to hear what God is speaking within, and to let Him work in and through me. As long as I stay in that "walk with God," there is no room for self-centeredness or boredom, only joy and satisfaction in the certainty that each of us is truly loved.

God has surely connected us, as if by a silken thread. He has weaved us into what has sometimes been called "the mystical Body of Christ." So much is missed when we act like single units. Why do we not hone in more to that connectedness, letting God use it?

<u>Endnote</u>: Following Ed's retirement from banking, he and his wife, Shirley, found opportunities to help others in various ways. One of those ways for Ed came through his volunteering for hospice. He sat with people who were mostly bedridden, which offered hours of respite to their caregivers.

Ed and I spoke of this work at times. Within one conversation, he said, "I never knew, as a banker, that at some point I would one day change the diaper of a dying person." Ed's heart was deeply committed to any assignment given to him while being with patients. He smiles as he says, "This is not something I was expected to do as a hospice volunteer. But, sometimes a circumstance arose wherein there was no other good choice."

During our last conversation, before his own cancer experience that led to death, Ed said, "As a banker, God used the goodness He placed in my heart to help people meet their financial needs. This became the focus of my life within my career at the bank. At times, I had to pit my ability and skills against factors within a 'bank gone wrong,' exerting the needed corrections. During those times, I prayed for God's guidance, and found that guidance. In each instance, circumstances were changed because of God's help. But, in hospice volunteer work, I depend on God's help in different ways. In the end, being at the bedside of dying people became the high point of my work life. There was so much love given in return for the time I spent with them. I kept remembering, 'God is love.'"

~~~

As believers, there is more for us than we have ever dreamed. The Lord's intent is to heal our souls of all that holds us back from being an expression of His presence on earth. The Lord wants to exhibit through us what truth looks like when it walks and talks. He will lead each of us as we listen, move forward, and follow God's guidance with due diligence.

We are to be a "peculiar" people, different from those who have their sights only on what the world can give them. We are chosen by God. What a privilege it is to hear and to answer God's call to be His friend and His servant.

We are a people *in progress*. God wants to move us onward toward "the prize," of receiving all God has for us...becoming what He knew we could be at the moment of our conception. The Apostle Paul called us "partakers of the heavenly calling" (Heb. 3:1).

If you have heard the Lord's call, "Follow me. I will make you fishers of men," the greatest of all adventures lies ahead. I pray for each person who finishes this book, to desire to forsake all that stands between you and healing, and the growth of your soul. I am with you as an imperfect human being, knowing the cross each of us is called to carry consists of the call of Christ to serve God through serving others...which means we seriously watch to keep our spirits clean. In this way, we are ready for when the voice of the Lord says, "This is the way, walk in it."

Addendums

Joy and Freedom	98
Dealing with Difficult Emotions: Finding Emotional Freedom	101
To Err is Human, to Forgive Divine	105
Help with Granting Forgiveness	108
Tips for Teaching Children How to Identify what They are Feeling	110
Tears: How They Help the Body Heal, as Well as the Soul	112
Are You Suffering from False Guilt?	115
Inner Healing Exercise	117
Journaling Sessions	118
Not Perfect, but Patient	123
Healing Affirmation	128
An Invitation	129

Joy and Freedom

The road to emotional freedom has bumps and detours. Reaching peace and happiness involves effort, yet rewards can be gained beyond what is thought possible.

The drawing, here, was done by a caricature artist at an open house attended a few years back. The only thing this artist knew about me was that I am a chaplain. Yet, in less than five minutes, I saw

him portray the spiritual journey. It's like *the ride* takes place on a tricycle with training wheels. As much as we would like to have a Harley experience, that just isn't there for us when it comes to healing the wounds of the past and learning how to appropriate—as fully as possible—God's truths intended for our lives. We do this in <u>slow mo</u>!

Although this is true, once we get a taste of the freedom that comes with healing our emotional wounds, we are not likely to turn back. And, if we set our wills to deal with difficult emotions, while doing continual forgiveness work, joy springs forth from the soul. Why? Because, we can't put a lid on our difficult feelings without also capping off most of our joy as well. As we reckon with feelings that are difficult to handle, versus pushing those down deep inside, we find our joy coming forth, as we have much for which to praise God. Soon, more and more excitement, enthusiasm, gladness, and peace of heart are present. Here is the key to living a life of emotional freedom. This is where we live on "the celebration side." *Voile! The Harley experience arrives.*

Through the ages, wisdom has flowed to humanity. Socrates once said, "Know thyself." He knew well that "the life which is unexamined is not worth living." Centuries later, William Shakespeare wrote, "To thine own self be true." These writers urge us to examine our hearts. King David's words, after he looked within, are common to my own. He cried out, "Create in me a clean heart, O God; and renew a right spirit within me." The greatest of all wisdom comes to play when, after examining, we align our lives with what God wants of us. With God's help, our hearts are made clean, and we are back on "the concrete" of righteous living wherein we respect ourselves, enjoy others, and abide within God's intentions.

There are numerous passages in the Bible that tell us to rejoice. If we, as believers, can't rejoice, but instead live and act as if life on earth is of primary importance, we are not living in truth. This world is only a brief part of eternal existence. We are just passing through. Life here, presents us with an opportunity to learn how to become more and more deeply involved with the Lord, our Creator. It is within this wonderful privilege that we hear God's call as to how we can best develop our gifts in ways that make the best of ourselves and serve the needs of our families and others.

Jesus talked much about joy, even under the shadow of the cross. *We are meant to enjoy our lives.*[20] And, for sure, there is joy in the presence of the Lord. We can feel that joy and that Presence while reading Scripture. Within those pages, the character and wondrous nature of God shows up. Joy can't help but arise when we capture some of the essence of what God and His goodness is about. It is easy to rejoice once we realize messages such as Philippians 4:4-7, are right on track–and put them to practice:

> "Rejoice in the Lord always. I will say it again: Rejoice! Let your gentleness be evident to all. The Lord is near. Do not be anxious about anything, but in everything, by prayer and petition, with thanksgiving, present your requests to God. And the peace of God, which transcends all understanding, will guard your hearts and your minds in Christ Jesus. Finally, brothers, whatever is true, whatever is noble, whatever is right, whatever is pure, whatever is lovely, whatever is admirable–if anything is excellent or praiseworthy–think about such things" (Phil 4:4-7).

---

[20] John 16:24, John 10:10, I Peter 1:8, Psalm 5:11, John 16:22. (These are just a few of the passages telling us of the joy intended for us.)

Joy Le Page Smith

Dealing with Difficult Emotions: Finding Emotional Freedom

Few people realize that validating their emotions is one of the best things they can do for their physical health, as well as for their emotional and mental health. Many people fear their emotions, as they don't know how to manage them. Many are even ashamed when the "not-so-good feelings" come up. But, having emotions that feel good and those that feel bad is part of being human. Feelings are neither right nor wrong. They just are.

Dr. Gordon Mate, author of *When the Body Says No*,[21] warns that serious health problems result when difficult emotions are ignored. For this reason, it is wise to reverse that pattern and avoid such vulnerability. We can pay attention to what is thought and felt. This allows us to identify our perceptions of what is happening, while also scrutinizing existing beliefs that may need changing.

Although this work takes time and effort, the payoff is great. For me, the work sees me having no more bouts with life-threatening illnesses. Those many hospital stays are behind me! And, I have much less stress.

It doesn't matter what age we are—young or old—our bodies are negatively impacted by stress when we are unable to acknowledge our emotions. Whether we do this work privately or with a counselor, it is vitally important to address our pain in life. However, only close, trusted friends and certain caring family members are interested in hearing about our difficult emotions. Others have their own to deal with. Choosing the right person as a confidant brings a sense of safety.

Dr. Mate makes a case for believing we will live longer and enjoy better physical health if we honor and identify our emotions. He writes, "The single greatest risk factor for death—and especially for

---

[21] Gabor Mate, *When the Body Says No* (New Jersey: John Wiley & Sons, Inc., 2003).

cancer death—was what the researchers called 'rationality and anti-emotionality or R/A.'" This state-of-being happens for a person when only good feelings are allowed to the exclusion of dealing with difficult feelings. With "rationality and anti-emotionality," most of a person's thought life is lived out in the left hemisphere of the brain where logic and analytical abilities formulate. For the most part, it is the right hemisphere of the brain that involves our emotions. So, it is the right hemisphere of the brain that many people are inclined to stifle. Dr. Mate calls the inability to handle difficult emotions a "hyper-rational, non-emotional coping style." Unfortunately, this pattern of denying difficult emotions results in considerable personal loss: Loss of emotionality, receptivity, creativity, and even a loss of health.

What needs to be done to reach good emotional health is clear. It takes noticing when something happens about which you don't feel good. Then, run a check with yourself asking, What is it that I am feeling? Am I hurt about this? "Or, sad about this?" Am I frustrated? Irritated? Disappointed? Am I angry? Does this cause me to fear? Is guilt what I am feeling?"

The first step toward healing is to decide we have a right to feel. The second step comes through taking the time to identify exactly what it is that we are feeling. The third step is having the courage to prayerfully seek to know what lies beneath these difficult feelings. This enables us to see where we need to grow and to be healed.

It is essential to realize that anger and hurt go together. When we are angry, there is also hurt involved. When we are hurt, there is always an element of anger that accompanies that pain. Underneath hurt and anger lies fear. Power to succeed in this work comes through telling God specifically what we are feeling. Then, purposely releasing each difficult emotion to God. The subconscious mind releases more easily when we mentally "see" all these is emotions moving away from us, while initiating strong resolve to be done with them.

The Lord is our elder brother in Scripture. We can envision God's work in our lives through picturing Jesus at work in the process. This aspect is excellent, as the act of imaging something mentally allows the healing work to reach the subconscious mind which works with pictures. We see this through the way the subconscious sends us dreams. So, this part of our being needs pictures in order to get on board with what we want. Creating mental pictures that show the subconscious mind the desired goal will bring the desired results more readily.

It helps to think of an upside-down triangle while doing this work. The illustration on the following page shows that when we have anger, we have hurt. And, when we have hurt, we have anger. Both are present when either one of these emotions is felt. Remember, healing takes place much more surely when we engage the subconscious mind with pictures, visualizations, and even diagrams.

For a printable version of this diagram, go to www.healing-with-Joy.com.

The Chaplain is in: Journey to Health and Happiness

The Way to Emotional Freedom

Anger is present when hurt is experienced. Conversely, hurt is felt when anger is experienced. Identify and release both of these emotions. In the end, identifying and releasing the fear beneath these two emotions is the crucial step

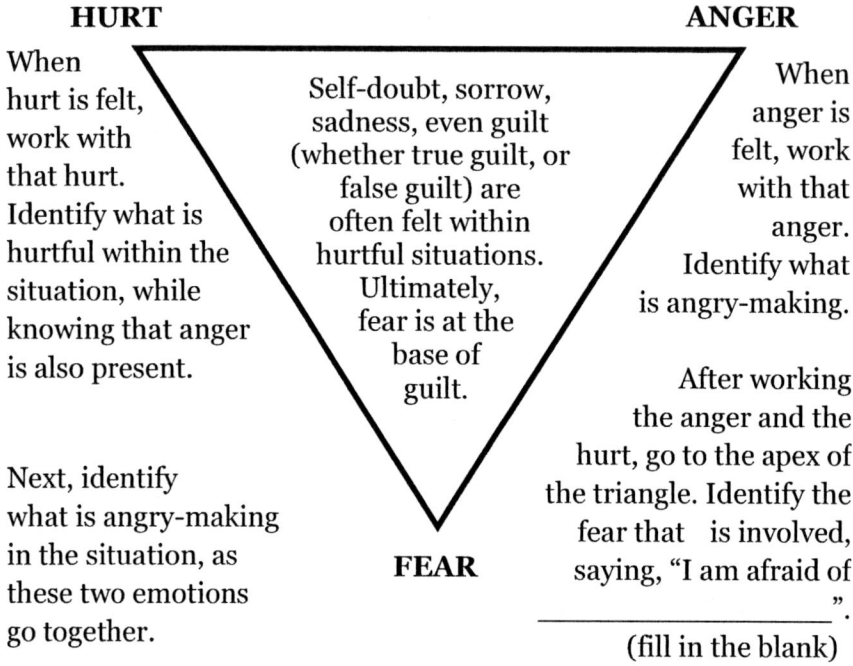

HURT

When hurt is felt, work with that hurt. Identify what is hurtful within the situation, while knowing that anger is also present.

Next, identify what is angry-making in the situation, as these two emotions go together.

Self-doubt, sorrow, sadness, even guilt (whether true guilt, or false guilt) are often felt within hurtful situations. Ultimately, fear is at the base of guilt.

FEAR

ANGER

When anger is felt, work with that anger. Identify what is angry-making.

After working the anger and the hurt, go to the apex of the triangle. Identify the fear that is involved, saying, "I am afraid of _____".

(fill in the blank)

Mentally lift the hurt, the anger, the guilt, and the fear that are felt within a situation, by identifying each emotion separately. Then release each one, **by forgiving** the person, or the circumstance involved. **Forgiving is a process.** Keep working the process each time a memory, or new happenstance reminds you of the emotional pain felt. Given time and effort, you will find the memory of that past event holds little, or no, discomfort for you. If this process becomes habitual, it is possible to live in emotional freedom, day-by-day. Forgiving is the ultimate key to emotional freedom. Holding on to hurt, anger, fear, and guilt creates excess baggage, reduces your energy, and adversely affects both your body and your psyche (soul).

"To Err Is Human, to Forgive Divine."
Alexander Pope

When we trust in the abiding presence of Jesus Christ living within, we hold the power to forgive. It takes working through our emotions, submitting each one to the Lord as it arises. Some wrongs are harder to forgive than others. Yet, without exception, God will make it possible when we determine not to hold a grudge against another—or ourselves.

That does not mean we have to continue spending time with a person who insists on bringing toxicity into our lives. Poison and injury can come through negativity and dishonesty. We can establish boundaries with those behaviors that hurt our lives. Forgiving does not mean we accept damaging behavior. With the Lord's help, we can separate the person from the behavior. This means we hold God's love in our hearts for the person, yet will not tolerate bad behavior. God gives us that kind of strength and empowerment.

Forgiving ourselves for things we have done that brings harm to others or to our own bodies is the hardest work of all. A young man, whom I will call "Lloyd," came to me with the sorrow of making a mistake that hurt another. He wept with shame, saying, "I've been a Christian since childhood. I just can't believe what I've done!"

I encouraged his tears, telling him, "Tears help us heal."

After giving space to what he was feeling, I asked, "Why do you think Christ allowed the Roman soldiers to nail him to the cross? By his own confession He could have called a legion of angels to save him."

Lloyd thought for several minutes before saying, "He did it to be our Savior."

I then asked, "When you think of Jesus choosing to die—embracing the role of Sacrificial Lamb wherein he could put an end to the practice of shedding the blood of innocent animals for the sake of human sin—how does it work for you?"

"I have always believed I will have eternal life through believing in Christ who offered Himself on my behalf," Lloyd responded.

"What does it do for you right now, in this moment, Lloyd?" I asked.

"Well, it gives me a lot of peace when I trust in it," He replied.

"Can you trust that Christ has forgiven the mistake you made?"

"In a spiritual sense, yes. But I do feel guilty for what I've done."

"And shame?"

"Yes—and I'm humiliated!"

"Do you think you might be dealing with pride?" I asked. "Thinking we have more holiness and more strength than we actually do have, is pride. Once we repent after making a mistake, it takes humbling ourselves before God, reckoning with how much we need the Lord's help moment-by- moment, in order to live this Christian life."

Lloyd pondered for a few moments. I waited while he absorbed the truth of this, making it his own. Then he said, "How can I continue to be a witness to the good news of Christ after blowing it in such a huge way?"

I responded, "Lloyd, I have blown it, too. Every Christian has in some way disgraced herself or himself. Are we depending on ourselves, or are we depending on God to be the Perfector of our faith, the Redeemer of our souls?"

"I see what you are saying," Lloyd said, "yet I could be seen as a hypocrite now. I have been a good witness until now. I don't want to pretend to be something when it is a proven fact I have fallen on my face!"

I responded, "If you or I witness our faith, it does not mean we are proclaiming to be Christ, Lloyd. The truth is that Christ lives in us and is perpetually saving us from our sins. We don't have to keep sinning. And, we don't have to tell everyone what sins we have done. Sometimes a mistake is so blatantly obvious that we are humiliated in front of our loved ones. Even then, we can praise God and thank Him for what we are about to learn from the experience. Being human calls for growth in understanding our weaknesses and our faults. We grow in humility as we recognize that we aren't what we thought we were, namely strong and reliable.

"As for continuing to minister to others, we can do it from our weakness. We can live a life of gratitude–knowing we are forgiven sinners. This is a much better place to be than to take pride in ourselves, thinking we have it all together, which would hardly bring lasting ministry to anyone," I concluded.

As we ended our time together, Lloyd and I prayed. When we finished, the look on his face showed joy, peace, and strength. The joy Lloyd felt came from knowing the relief that comes from taking that trip back to Christ on the cross. I have done it often myself. It is there that we receive the power to forgive others for the hurt and harm we have experienced through them.

> *"Trust not yourself, but your defects to know.*
> *Make use of every friend and every foe."*
> Alexander Pope (1688-1744)

Help With Granting Forgiveness

<u>Why do the work it takes to forgive?</u>

1. We begin to feel better, as we have less emotional pain to manage in our daily lives.

2. Our relationships have potential to change.

3. We physically release the toxicity that builds up in our cells due to emotional anguish. Hurt, sadness, fear, anger, and bitterness held within does, over time, affect our health. Forgiving ourselves for our mistakes and our poor choices releases the guilt that can do a nasty number on our health.

4. We feel the "atta girl" or "atta boy" over doing what God asks of us. This places us in the Creator's will and brings a satisfying feeling to our souls. This emotion promotes health: physically, mentally, emotionally, and spiritually.

<u>Points to consider as regards forgiving</u>

1. Some people think forgiving shows weakness. The opposite is true. It takes a great deal of strength to forgive some people. And, it takes considerable determination and strength to forgive some things that have happened to us.

2. People often think forgiving means they are condoning bad, hurtful, or spiteful behaviors. The truth is that forgiving a person does not mean the behavior is accepted; not at all. To forgive is to release your soul from the difficult emotions that result when you are hurt or harmed. It means you let God be God. This frees God to work on the person or people involved, especially when you pray for them. Jesus taught not only to forgive, but also to pray for our enemies. To forgive means setting yourself free of emotional bondage.

3. Forgiving is a process. Initially, we set our will to forgive. Later, when old memories surface, or something current reminds

us of what happened in the past, we deal with the feelings of hurt, anger, and fear that arise. This takes getting clear about what is at the base of the feelings. Then we tell God, "I give you these emotions. I release them to you. I have forgiven this." The process takes as long as it takes. We have to be patient with ourselves, doing the work as many times as it becomes necessary.

4. The grace of God fills the soul of a person who determines to forgive all that has hurt or harmed him or her. This brings to us "the peace that passes understanding." Aside from living in God's will, nothing else in life can bring this level of peace. We accept God's peace, even when we cannot understand that *peace can exist within difficult circumstances.*

5. We are not asked to forgive others because God demands obedience. God asks us to forgive others, even our enemies, because *we are loved.* God wants us to have the best possible life!

The bottom line as regards forgiveness

To have the ultimate in life, means we will seek to live in the kingdom of God. Ours is a spiritual kingdom that Jesus brought to us through His teachings. This kingdom presents a very different way of living from the way usually seen within the world. The kingdom of God is all about loving and being loved. It is about being led by a heart filled with God's Holy Spirit. This state-of-being sees us doing good for our families, and finding ways to serve others through using our gifts, our talents. While making the lives of others better, we are benefiting as well. The joy of the Lord becomes a growing entity in our souls!

The Chaplain is in: Journey to Health and Happiness

Tips for Teaching Children How to Identify What They Are Feeling

Dr. Gordon Mate, author of *When the Body Says No*, states that children who hold their emotions in rigidly are taxing their nervous systems. When the adults in their lives discourage their expressing difficult emotions, children have no other recourse than to hold in their anger and sadness, ever so tightly. Dr. Mate connects serious illness, in some instances, with the fact that the nervous system only has so much energy to expend for "pushing down powerful emotions that cry out for expression."

Below is a technique to use with children, which will help them validate their emotions. This will result in their having less stress and better health. When a child is upset, ask, "What are you feeling?"

Mostly, both big people and little people have to learn how to validate emotions through identifying what is felt and how the feeling relates to what is happening in life. The key to success within this work is to watch when you feel uncomfortable or unhappy about something said or done. Then do the work of identifying what emotion is arising.

The following five simple steps will give children a method for identifying what it is they are feeling:

Hold up one of your hands with your palm open toward your face. Look at your fingers. Let your first four fingers represent a feeling: glad, sad, mad, and "afrad." (The word "afraid" is tweaked here to allow a rhyme.) In this exercise your thumb can represent guilt. My suggestion is to present these steps to your children, helping them to memorize the process. The idea, here, is to get the children to identify their feelings and feel O.K. about expressing them, rather than to act out their feelings.

Step 1: Beginning with your little finger, say, "glad," while deciding whether or not this is the emotion you are feeling.

Probably, you aren't feeling glad in the midst of a difficult moment. Yet, this little finger (our glad finger) can remind us that within every difficult circumstance we can find something for which to be glad or grateful.

Step 2: Move to your ring finger and say, "sad," while asking yourself, "Am I feeling sad? Have I been hurt by this thought of mine or by what has happened just now?" *Our negative thoughts can hurt as much as words from others.* Watch for them and weed them out as quickly as they come. Negative thoughts pull you down and are self-destructive.

Step 3: Next hold up your middle finger and say, "mad," as this is one of our frequent feelings. Keep in mind that irritation and frustration are derivatives of anger. Ask, "Am I frustrated? Am I irritated?"

Step 4: Now, hold up your index finger and say "afrad" (afraid). Consider the emotion of fear by asking yourself, "Am I feeling fear or anxiety in this situation?"

Step 5: End with your thumb, saying, "My thumb stands for guilt." Ask yourself, "Is guilt what I am feeling within this situation?" And, thumbs *up for overcoming all guilt.*

Tears: How They Help the Body Heal, as Well as the Soul

It is said, "healing the soul is like peeling an onion." This is true. The layers of pain, resentment, bitterness, and sorrow come off one by one. No matter how many conferences attended and books read in hopes of getting more comfortable in our skins, most of us come to a notable realization: The hidden pain in our psyches hasn't gone away. It takes more than understanding. We are going to have to deal with it.

Here is the crux of the matter: If we want to be whole, we have to fight against all inclinations to gulp down feelings. Instead, when we feel tears at the corners of our eyes, we must *admit* what we are feeling, then *allow* the tears to flow, in a place where we feel safe. Most often, this takes place in privacy. Without a doubt, your body and your soul are healthier when you let those tears flow. Trust this natural, God-given process. Remind yourself that this emotional work does pay off. Freedom from your inner pain is on the way. Days of living with less stress lie ahead. Learning to grieve life's losses in this manner was a major factor in my becoming well after having to wage a serious battle to stay alive.

My "Get Well Program" involved praying, meditating, and studying Scriptures. However, I also journaled and listened to my dreams. One dream in particular spoke loud and clear about all my inner angst. In this dream, I am shown a huge mountain of frozen tears. The dream scene is an awesomely cold place! I awaken knowing that a piece of truth has paid me a visit. I see, clearly, that a mountain of frozen tears resides within my psyche. Those frozen tears need to come down, but they have to come down slowly, not all at once. I have to own up to all that stored grief, now so remote and hard to reach.

Eventually, my mountain of frozen tears began to thaw, allowing me to feel and to release that old, buried pain. I learned the value of tears and the need to let them have their way when they want to come. Jesus said, "You will know the truth and the truth will set you free" (Jn 8:32). The fact remains that *coming to truth* can take a lot of time and diligent effort when we have repressed a great deal of emotion, hoping it will "go away"--if we just stay busy enough. Or, drink enough ... do enough drugs ... recreate more. Clearly, if we want the change which brings a better life--one that is honoring to God--we have to do the work. And, for a lot of us, tears are part of it.

The truth about tears is that they help to heal our psyche (soul). And, amazingly enough, this little bit of water that begs to run down our faces *helps our bodies.*

Science indicates that tears are always present in the eyes and contain water, mucins, proteins, oils and electrolytes to keep the eyes moist, protect the eyes and facilitate the smooth movement of the lids over the surface. Tears are essential and their functions are many.

William H. Frey II, Ph.D. and Muriel Langseth, are authors of *Crying: The Mystery of Tears.*[22] Dr. Frey, a neuroscientist, at the Regions Hospital in St. Paul, Minnesota, suggests that physical benefits are gained through releasing emotional tears. He studied tears for 15 years, analyzing two types: 1) tears that come while crying when we are emotionally upset or stressed; and 2) tears arising from eye irritants, including onions. Dr. Frey and his colleagues also found that all tears are not the same and that stress-induced tears have a 24% higher protein concentration than tears caused by eye irritants. Dr. Frey proposed that weeping is an excretory process which facilitates the removal of substances that build up during times of emotional stress.

One of the compounds found by Dr. Frey and his colleagues in human tears is Adrenocorticotropic Hormone (ACTH). This chemical is known to increase in the blood during stress. Dr. Frey's studies demonstrate that 85% of women and 73% of men feel better after crying. This indicates that suppressing tears over

---

[22] William H. Frey, Muriel Langseth, *The Mystery of Tears* (Minneapolis: Winston Press, 1977).

long periods of time may reduce our ability to alleviate stress, while increasing our risk of stress-related disorders, which include high blood pressure, heart problems, certain ulcers, and perhaps even memory loss.

More and newer research is showing that our bodies are helped when we pay attention to those moments when we feel tears arising, or when we have a lump in the throat. On an Internet site, Nurse Connect, in a posting titled "Nursing Dynamics and Clinical Issues," a nurse writes: "Without tears most nurses would be emotional wrecks. Let's face it, nursing is an emotional profession; on any given day we may witness pain, suffering and death, or extreme joy, relief and gratitude ... encouraging a colleague not to cry, to 'be strong,' is detrimental to their psyche." This nurse verifies that chemicals built up in the body during stressful moments are removed by tears. We all have challenges, disappointments, and stressful times. Yielding to a good cry is a definite way of lowering our stress level and potentially helping our bodies to release harmful stress-related chemicals.

Ultimately, allowing our tears permits both physical and emotional benefits. For one, tears carry a promise for better times ahead. We can be certain that clarity about what is at the root of our sadness, confusion or anxiety brings a certain joy of its own. Progress is gained and we are encouraged to keep moving forward with increased understanding about how to help our bodies stay healthy.

Are You Suffering from False Guilt?

There is guilt that truly belongs to us. And, there is false guilt. Here is a look at the difference between them. First, there is true guilt. For instance, a young man, we will call A.J., was driving with several friends in his car. They had been drinking. He was enjoying his friends when suddenly A.J. hit another car. The other driver was injured. There is no question about A.J.'s behavior. He was truly guilty of driving while under the influence of alcohol.

Another American young man, B.W., married a woman from Brazil, named A.T. (again, not the person's true initials). There were cultural differences and neither he nor his new wife could reconcile the differences that came up daily for the couple. They sought counseling; yet, after giving five years to the marriage, the two of them were fighting nearly every day. They could agree on one thing. The two decided to divorce. B.W., however, could not shake the feeling of guilt. He had grown up in a church that said divorce should never happen. In fact, he was taught that people are sent to hell for the sin of divorce. B.W. suffered a great amount of inner turmoil, thinking he, somehow, could have made the marriage work.

As the years passed, he was helped by attending a church where divorce was looked at differently. The pastor told him, "Divorce is kind, if it ends something cruel. God forgives us when we make choices that are less than best." B.W. knew that continuing in his marriage would have been cruel to himself, and that would also be true for his wife. The guilt was still felt until he came to my office for counseling. After a few sessions, B.W. could see his patterns of feeling guilty about a lot of happenings in his life. He learned the difference between feeling guilty for a wrong action, and feeling guilty out of a tendency to be overly responsible. He forsook the teaching of his childhood that caused him to fear going to hell for having a divorce in his life. B.W. found freedom in realizing that:

1) God heals our lives from brokenness when we ask for God's help, 2) When we forsake wrong behaviors, God forgives our wrong doings, never to hold them against us, and 3) Mistakes become our teachers when we purpose to learn from them.

For sure, God does not want us to live with guilt of any kind. "Come now, let us reason together," says the Lord. "Though your sins are like scarlet, they shall be as white as snow; though they are red as crimson, they shall be like wool" (Isa 1:18).

We learn how to defeat false guilt by recognizing it, then releasing it. We can say, "My spirit is done with that" each time we see the pattern of being responsible for something that is out of our control. Below is a list that includes a few of the tendencies that reveal a pattern for carrying false guilt. If you own up to even one of these tendencies, you are dealing with false guilt. Now, you can begin to weed out all messages within your thought life that support this unhealthy pattern.

1. I worry daily about my actions, and my choices.
2. I feel responsible when things go wrong.
3. I'm always blaming myself.
4. I'm *often* apologizing; saying, "I'm sorry" (to the point of overuse).
5. I care a lot about what others think of me.
6. I find it hard to say "no" to others.

"False guilt comes from saying no to people... The only true guilt comes from saying no to God."
From Paul Tournier's *Guilt and Grace.*

Inner Healing Exercise

When the experiences of life are difficult and painful, you may find this exercise is very helpful.

For best results, lie down (or sit quietly) envisioning the entirety of your torso covered by a huge sponge. See the Lord Jesus placing this sponge on your body, holding it there. Envision Him as sending love into your soul.

Next, purpose to let go the difficult feelings while visualizing them being released from your body into the sponge. (I visualize vapors leaving my body while releasing the feelings.) Do this as long and as often as you need to while letting go of the pain you are feeling.

The subconscious mind works with pictures, images created by dreams, or by our creating them consciously. For this reason, an exercise such as this allows the message of healing to be received by the subconscious mind *where healing is needed.*

If you let tears flow when they arise, this will help you release the painful emotions, and bless your body with relief. Tell yourself that love is flowing like a river into your heart and throughout your entire body, replacing the pain. Offer thanks to God as you receive this healing.

This healing work is a process; it takes varying degrees of time, depending on the depth of the pain.

I find the exercise even more helpful when it is possible to fall asleep within the process of releasing the pain. This allows the healing to move deeper into the subconscious mind where healing is needed.

Journaling Sessions

Once while attending an eight-day silent retreat, I discovered the edge of my comfort zone, a boundary beyond which I did not want God to go. As I examined this boundary with the help of my spiritual director, I found it was comprised of fear. I was afraid that if I committed myself more fully to God, He would ask something of me that I was not able, or willing, to give. I also feared the unknown. Would moving beyond this established boundary make me so "spiritual" that my husband, and other friends, could not enjoy my company? Would it affect the way I related to others?

God could not get any further with me until I was willing to *work through my fears*. Thankfully, my spiritual director spoke truth into my life, providing the ground on which my fears could crumble.

He said, "Joy, God is a passionate lover. Yet, God loves you and will never do anything to hurt your life. It is safe to trust God." Somehow I knew, from that point on, that God would only bring good changes into my life.

Strengthened and freed by that truth, I relinquished my fears and moved on to experience new and wondrous depths in prayer. I gained more comprehension of the unfathomable love of God. Many years have passed and I have not had a single regret in this matter, but I have also been filled with awe, many times, by how the Lord *rewards* me for believing and trusting enough to give up my *lock and keys*. How marvelous is this spiritual journey!

Exercise #1

Before beginning this exercise, please read the following Scripture passages: I Jn 4:18, Jas 4:8 and II Tim 1:7.

Please open the exercises with a prayer (use the words below, or your own, if you prefer).

Heavenly Father, I do not understand your ways. My thoughts are so far from Your thoughts. How can I comprehend the love and mercy You have extended? Open my eyes that I might see and understand. I want to believe that You have only good in store for me, that You know what is best, and that giving Your will preeminence above my own desires bring the greatest possible happiness in this life and the next.

Lord, I do believe. Please help me with encroaching unbelief that plagues me at times. I ask for Your help, as I desire to relinquish my fears in order that You can work Your will in my life, unhindered. I want to know You and to more fully comprehend Your truths. Take my hand, take my heart. Be the Lover of my soul. Then, my sentiments for You, uniting with the great love You have for me, will break down fear's boundaries and eradicate its pervasive confinements. Thank You for being patient with me, as You always are, always have been, and ever shall be. For it is Your nature to do so. As I learn more and more about abiding in You, I trust Your nature. Lord, Your will be mine through the work Your Holy Spirit is doing within me. Amen.

Journaling:

Step 1: Make a list of the people who have been most inspiring or helpful in your life. Include the *heroes*, meaning the teachers and closest friends, those who you find vividly ensconced in your memory. Next, carefully identify the characteristics each one of these individuals possesses. Put these in a separate column beside their names.

Now, let your mind linger on these characteristics, forming a portrait of the Father, the One who created us. Each of these characteristics (each talent, gift, or ability we admire, or benefit gained from others) was first a part of God, imparted to humans for the common good of all.

You may want to stay with the exercise for as long as possible, even up to an hour. Fill column after column with all the characteristics and giftedness you have ever seen or heard of in human beings. Then, as you try to envision One Being with all these benefits, you have moved closer to comprehending God, whom Jesus knew as "Father." Trust and understanding will expand as you work with this exercise.

Step 2: Savor long moments with this wondrous Being. This is to contemplate, wordlessly, the awesomeness of embracing what is truly only a finite glimpse into God's personhood, the one who is Parent of all Parents, Creator of Life, Light, and Love.

Step 3: During the coming days and weeks, consider this thought: Within each one who walks this earth, there is a little bit of God waiting to be discovered. This goodness, once seen, can touch your soul with great joy.

Conclusion of Exercise #1

Write a letter of appreciation to God for the goodness that you know exists in yourself. If you find resistance to this part of the exercise, due to a fear of being prideful, consider this definition of humility: "Knowing fully what you <u>are</u>, as well as what you are not." God made us, and all that God has made is *good*.

Exercise #2

Step 1: Spend 1/2 hour in a quiet place, with a piece of paper and a pen. Take several days to complete this exercise, if you wish. Use 15 minutes for each of the four exercises below. It is best to do only one each day for four days, while not working beyond the 15 minutes suggested. Complete the sentences below by filling in the blanks. Following each of the four emotions, write as many entries as come to mind. On the following day, either continue working with that same emotion, or go on to another emotion.

Continue with the exercise for as many days as it takes to feel finished.

1. **I feel angry because**_____

2 **I feel hurt because**_____

3. **I feel fearful (or anxious) about** _____

4. **I feel guilty because**_____

As you work with each of the above efforts, be sure to stop at the end of 15 minutes. Then ask God for the grace and the ability to release the painful emotion and to submit it to God. Pray to be empowered with the ability to forgive the painful events of your life, along with all persons who have hurt you. Ask God to forgive your failures and to strengthen you in your ability to forgive yourself for every poor choice and bad behavior, while releasing any felt guilt.

Sometimes we feel guilty when we are not truly guilty. We *are* guilty when we have intended to do harm, or when we have thoughtlessly hurt another by being inconsiderate of his or her feelings and needs. See Addendum on page 115 titled "Are You Suffering from False Guilt" for more coverage on this subject.

Ask for God's help as you give up all fears you listed in #3 above. In the future, form a habit of admitting your fears to God when they present themselves, choosing to believe that God loves you and is there (and will be there) for you in the midst of all your needs. Tell yourself: "There is nothing I need to fear." Use this affirmation anytime you are fearful. Breathe away the emotion, releasing it, each time the emotion is felt. Do the same when you feel anxiety.

Step 2: Complete the following sentence while making as many entries as you can within a 15 minute time frame:

I am thankful because _____

Conclusion of Exercise #2

Stop all thoughts, or mental pictures, bringing your mind to a state of inner quietude. Sit, basking in the truth that God loves you very much. It may help to think of this experience as being like sitting in the warmth of the sun. Let the truth that you are loved by God go deep into your psyche (soul). Sense your spirit as being united with God...rest...and let God cradle your being.

When words or pictures come to mind, let them go. Nothing else is important during these 15 minutes, except for feeling united with God. (During this part of the exercise, take more time, if doing so feels appropriate for you.)

You may be amazed at the results if you use the above prayer form early, before starting each day. Make notes about any subtle, or not so subtle, changes that have transpired for you. Share with a trusted friend or spiritual mentor what takes place for you as you complete these exercises. In so doing, you will more fully validate your spiritual and emotional advancements.

Joy Le Page Smith

Not Perfect - But Patient!

It was my night for a 24-hour rotation at the hospital where I was a student chaplain in Clinical Pastoral Education. During these on-call nights, it is necessary for the chaplain to cover calls to the emergency department, trauma center and to attend all codes. When a code is called, you know a patient has died and that the medical team is rushing to do all possible to revive the person. A chaplain's role is to attend to the needs of the patient's family, offering emotional and spiritual help. This ministry often includes prayer. Yet above all, a chaplain's duties involve carefully discerning the best option for care within each particular circumstance for that specific family's needs. Afterwards, the chaplain's work includes determining the needs of the patient, provided the person has survived.

I greatly appreciated the fact that sleeping quarters were available, making it possible to rest at times during the night. Yet, on this particular night I was on duty 20 hours, with little rest, when I was called by a nurse to pray for a baby. No other information was given. I hurried to the floor with the room number in hand. In no way was I prepared to see what awaited there! A baby lay in a small crib, only this baby was born without a brain, or a skull. His head was as large and nearly as flat as a pancake. I was looking at a face that was transparent. Multiple blood vessels showed through his skin. His eyes rocked and shocked my soul with their upward stare.

Several realizations swirled through my head. For one, the knowledge that the shape and condition of this child's head meant no one could pick him up. He could not be held in his mother's arms, or register his father's face. Second, no medical expertise could resolve his need for a brain and a skull. Third, without a doubt his life was presenting a tremendous struggle for all involved. Over all these thoughts stood the knowledge that this little person could not live long like this and may well not receive nourishment. "Allowed to die," is, at times, a medical choice. I quieted my mind long enough to pray for the child and his parents, yet my heart was hot with anguish. How could such a thing happen to a tiny, innocent child?

I headed for the hospital chapel as fast as I could go through the hallways and down the elevator. Once there I knelt before the altar, my faith spinning like a wobbly top, slowly losing its momentum. How God? How is it that with all your power, and all the love we believe you have for us, how could you let this child come into life in such a condition as this? I knew, there on my knees, that I was engaging the same God that the suffering servant Job addressed when he raised his fists and shouted his questions. And, I remembered that God told Job he simply was not prepared to know all the ins and outs of creation. God expected Job to weave the suffering he experienced into the whole of life. As time passed at the chapel altar, I was humbled.

Still, the pain did not go away. I continued to carry this child's dilemma in my heart. My pain was based in fear, fear of living in a world that is so unpredictable and seemingly out of control. It was my duty to find this baby's parents and offer to help them through this startling and grief-filled time. When I thought I could face them, I looked throughout the hospital, but I could not find them.

As a student, I was still learning how to deal with extreme circumstance. Now, 18 years later, I would do things differently. I'd move heaven and earth until the parents were found so I could join them in their suffering. At least, I would do the one thing possible. I could go to them and weep with them. Right then, however, I was barely able to handle the total ineptness that had overtaken me. Since then, I have seen many more evidences that humanity carries with it inevitable imperfection and suffering. But right then, there was a lot weighing against my being able to stand before a mother and a father, knowing they had been given a child that had no mind ... born without the brain that gives the gift of knowing oneself, experiencing life and others. I was gripped by the fact this baby boy would have no thoughts, no emotions, no perceptions nor beliefs.

I could not talk about this to anyone. It was as if my soul

freeze-framed the incident. No doubt my psyche wanted to deny what is possible in this life. As I look back on this incident today, I feel some shame, sensing that I was weak and that perhaps another chaplain could have managed better. On the other hand, part of being effective with people is offering all of who we are, including our imperfections, and then to be patient with our failures.

At an earlier time in life, before training as a chaplain, I was impatient with life. I wanted to do more, find a mode of service that would do justice to my desire to minister to people in pain. How I longed to help others find the freedom of heart that comes through experiencing God's love within the greatest struggles of life. I had seen how God shows up within circumstances of great pain and sorrow. I longed to work with people, helping them get through their most difficult hours with the availability of God's help, when we but ask for it. Yet, I couldn't seem to get out of God's waiting room.

Then I met Hilda, a 73-year-old woman who sensed my frustration. She questioned me in a way that allowed this frustration to flow out. Her words were few, but well-placed and hit the mark.

"What's your hurry?" she asked.

"Fear," I answered. "Fear that my life will slip away and not amount to much."

Hilda stood tall and stalwart, looked me in the eye and said, "You have all of eternity."

It was incredulous to hear her say, "I've decided that I can wait." In her, I saw the rock of patience and I was thinking, "Yes, and you are about to run out of time!" As I sit here today, now nearly her age, I'm thinking she wasn't old at all!

Fortunately, the point she made was not lost. I recalled a time during the previous summer, while in the mountains and alone with God. I prayed lustfully," I'll do anything you ask ... clean toilets ... wash windows, or pots and pans, just open the door!" The truth about that prayer was that I was willing to do anything all right, except wait.

It is said about a song, "There is no music in the rest, but there is the making of music in the rest." After that talk with Hilda, I decided to put aside my impatience and to trust that what God wanted to do in my life would come in God's own good timing.

Within an hour after Hilda and I had talked, her husband Nandor handed me a book. At bedtime I read, "Much as I long to be out of here, I don't believe a single day has been wasted. What will come out of my time here it is too early to say. But something is bound to come of it ..." This was a quote from Dietrich Bonhoeffer's *Prisoner of God*, written from a German prison during his long stay prior to the day when he was executed for his faith within Hitler's regime. Many millions of us have read Dietrich Bonhoeffer's inspiring writings since the day he wrote those words in a prison cell.

Nandor knew nothing of Hilda's and my talk of an hour before. How perfect are God's ways, for those words of Bonhoeffer punctuated Hilda's words! When we really want to hear from God, we will, when we are willing to be patient and wait. Yet, waiting on God in life can surely test our patience at times. Surely, none of us like waiting when we are ready to move. What I came to realize without a doubt is that God's timing is always best, although God's timetable, rarely aligns with mine. Within the 10 years following that conversation with Hilda, much transpired within my family. I found myself fully focused on the needs of my loved ones. It is easy to see, in retrospect, how that was the best possible use of my time and talent during that period of my life. In hindsight, it is no surprise to realize how each difficult experience I've had in life has prepared me to be with others in extraordinary circumstances.

It is amazing how right the timing was when the door opened for me to enter Clinical Pastor Education at Good Samaritan Regional Hospital where I learned how best to serve the sick and the dying as a resident chaplain. Once certified, it was as if God took my hand and led me into Dr. Leslie Edison's practice at Moon Valley Medical Center. Since then, for the past 16 years, I have taken her referrals while rejoicing in the honor that comes to me through her trust. I continually sense the trust bestowed on me by those whom I serve. The lessons of life come slowly, yet surely. And, for sure, it pays to be patient.

Actually, the best way to be healthy in life is to be patient! And, who wants to be patient? Nobody that I know! Truth be told, attaining patience is a learned art. Letting patience "do her perfect work," as Scripture puts it, is the ultimate way to be whole, both emotionally and physically.

Healing Affirmation

I am loved ... I am wanted ...
I am treasured and cherished.

I was not born of the will of flesh but of
the will of God. God wanted me to be born.

My Father is rich in cattle and lands.
He holds the wealth of the world in His Hands.

I have nothing to fear. God is within me,
through the powerful Holy Spirit.

All is well with my soul ...
it's okay to laugh and to play.

All my sins are forgiven and I have been given the
free gift of eternal life with God in Heaven

At night before sleep:

I am precious ... I am a royal child of The King.
I am a partaker of the Kingdom of God within ...
I have righteousness, peace and joy in the Holy Spirit.

My heart is set on doing the will
of God. God's power within me will
win over all obstacles. I am not weak
but mighty and strong through God

An Invitation

Now you have heard my story and read some of my offerings. While reading, you may have thought of your own spiritual journey. Or, perhaps, you felt a "knock on your heart's door" inviting you to follow Jesus Christ. If so, I hope you will respond. It is just a matter of saying "yes" to that call felt within. People who do so know they are making a decision that will change their lives.

Most of us feel unworthy of God's favor. We think of our past mistakes and failures. Yet, all it takes is asking to be forgiven; then, *in an instant* our hearts are cleansed. From that moment on, the precious presence of God is there to awaken our spirits. God makes it simple for the journey to begin. Scripture says we "carry precious treasure in earthen vessels." Gradually, life is changed. And, we are no longer alone.

Here is a simple prayer in the event you find it helpful:

"Dear God, I desire to give You the contents of my heart--the good of it and the not so good of it. I accept the call of Jesus Christ and acknowledge Him as Your Son, my Savior. I believe you can strengthen me to the point wherein You, Lord, can use my gifts and my talents in the service of Your kingdom. As I surrender my heart, I pray *Your kingdom to come and for Your will to be done in my life. Amen.*"

The first thing to do, now, is to find other Christians who understand what you have just done and will help you grow in your Christian faith. Going to church will give you a family within this chosen walk with God. There are many churches to choose from. Visit until you feel welcomed and have a sense of, *"Yes! This is it,"* felt in your heart. Now, you will be at home. You will have opportunities for worship and also for studying the Bible. Here, you will gain rewarding connections with other believers.

What I've come to love most is listening to the stories of what takes place in the lives of individuals once they chose to make Jesus

Christ Lord of their lives. You too can tell your story as the Spirit prompts you, for you will indeed have a story to tell.

"Behold, I stand at the door and knock; if anyone

Hears My voice and opens the door,

I will come in to him and will dine with him,

and he with Me." (Rev. 3:20)

NOTES

NOTES

NOTES

NOTES

Joy Le Page Smith

NOTES

NOTES

**Visit Joy's website
for additional articles, blogs,
and Scriptural helps:**

http://www.healing-with-Joy.com

Additional copies of this book can be ordered from www.Amazon.com, or from your favorite online or neighborhood bookstore.